ISBN 978-1-330-03599-3
PIBN 10009670

1 MONTH OF
FREE
READING

at

www.ForgottenBooks.com

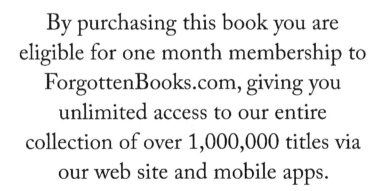

By purchasing this book you are eligible for one month membership to ForgottenBooks.com, giving you unlimited access to our entire collection of over 1,000,000 titles via our web site and mobile apps.

To claim your free month visit:

www.forgottenbooks.com/free9670

The Book of
BUSINESS ETIQUETTE

The Book of
Business Etiquette

Garden City   New York
Doubleday, Page & Company
1922

RESPECTFULLY INSCRIBED
(AS BEFITS AN AUTHOR)
TO
THREE BUSINESS MEN

ACKNOWLEDGMENT

IT WOULD be a pleasure to call over by name and thank individually the business men and the business organizations that so graciously furnished the material upon which this little book is based. But the author feels that some of them will not agree with all the statements made and the inferences drawn, and for this reason is unable to do better than give this meager return for a service which was by no means meager.

CONTENTS

PART I

PART I

THE BOOK OF BUSINESS ETIQUETTE

I

THE AMERICAN BUSINESS MAN

THE business man is the national hero of America, as native to the soil and as typical of the country as baseball or Broadway or big advertising. He is an interesting figure, picturesque and not unlovable, not so dashing perhaps as a knight in armor or a soldier in uniform, but he is not without the noble (and ignoble) qualities which have characterized the tribe of man since the world began. America, in common with other countries, has had distinguished statesmen and soldiers, authors and artists—and they have not all gone to their graves unhonored and unsung—but the hero story which belongs to her and to no one else is the story of the business man.

Nearly always it has had its beginning in humble surroundings, with a little boy born in a log cabin in the woods, in a wretched shanty at the edge of a field, in a crowded tenement section or in the slums of a foreign city, who studied and worked by daylight and firelight while he made his living blacking boots or selling papers until he found the trail by which he could climb to what we are pleased to call success.   Measured by the standards of Greece and Rome or the Middle Ages, when practically the only form of achievement worth mentioning was fighting to kill, his career has not been a romantic one.   It has had to do not with dragons and banners and trumpets, but with stockyards and oil fields, with railroads, sewer systems, heat, light, and water plants, telephones, cotton, corn, ten-cent stores and—we might as well make a clean breast of it —chewing gum.

We have no desire to crown the business man with a halo, though judging from their magazines and from the stories which they write of their own lives, they are almost without spot or blemish.   Most of them seem not even to have had faults to overcome.   They were born perfect.   Now the truth is that the methods of accomplishment which the American business man has used have not always been above reproach and still are not.   At the same time it would not be hard to prove that he—and here we are speaking of the average—with all his faults and failings (and they are many), with all his virtues (and he is not without them), is superior in character to the business men of other times in other countries. This without boasting. It would be a great pity if he were not.

Without trying to settle the question as to whether he is good or bad (and he really can be pigeon-holed no better than any one else) we have to accept this: He is the biggest factor in the American commonwealth to-day. It follows then, naturally, that what he thinks and feels will color and probably dominate the ideas and the ideals of the rest of the country. Numbers of our magazines—and they are as good an index as we have to the feeling of the general public—are given over completely to the service or the entertainment of business men (the T. B. M.) and an astonishing amount of space is devoted to them in most of the others.

It may be, and as a matter of fact constantly is, debated whether all this is good for the country or not. We shall not go into that. It has certainly been good for business, and in considering the men who have developed our industries we have to take them, and maybe it is just as well, as they are and not as we think they ought to be.

There was a time when the farmer was the principal citizen. And the politician ingratiated himself with the people by declaring that he too had split rails and followed the plow, had harvested grain and had suffered from wet spells and dry spells, low prices, dull seasons, hunger and hardship. This is still a pretty sure way to win out, but there are others. If he can refer feelingly to the days when he worked and sweated in a coal mine, in a printing shop, a cotton, wool, or silk mill, steel or motor plant, he can hold his own with the ex-farmer's boy. We have become a nation of business men. Even the "dirt" farmer has become a business man—he has learned that he not only has to produce, he must find a market for his product.

In comparing the business man of the present with the business man of the past we must remember that he is living in a more difficult world. Life was comparatively simple when men dressed in skins and ate roots and had their homes in scattered caves. They felt no need for a code of conduct because they felt no need for one another. They depended not on humanity but on nature, and perhaps human brotherhood would never have come to have a meaning if nature had not proved treacherous. She gave them berries and bananas, sunshine and soft breezes, but she gave them trouble also in the shape of wild beasts, and savages, terrible droughts, winds, and floods. In order to fight against these enemies, strength was necessary, and when primitive men discovered that two were worth twice as much as one they began to join forces. This was the beginning of civilization and of politeness. It rose out of the oldest instinct in the world—self-preservation.

When men first organized into groups the units were small, a mere handful of people under a chief, but gradually they became larger and larger until the nations of to-day have grown into a sort of world community composed of separate countries, each one supreme in its own domain, but at the same time bound to the others by economic ties stronger than sentimental or political ones could ever be. People are now more dependent on one another than they have ever been before, and the need for confidence is greater. We cannot depend upon one another unless we can trust one another.

The American community is in many respects the most complex the world has ever seen, and the hardest to manage. In other countries the manners have been the natural result of the national development. The strong who had risen to the top in the struggle for existence formed themselves into a group.   The weak who stayed at the bottom fell into another, and the bulk of the populace, which, then as now, came somewhere in between, fell into a third or was divided according to standards of its own.   Custom solidified the groups into classes which became so strengthened by years of usage that even when formal distinctions were broken down the barriers were still too solid for a man who was born into a certain group to climb very easily into the one above him.   Custom also dictated what was expected of the several classes.   Each must be gracious to those below and deferential to those above.   The king, because he was king, must be regal.   The nobility must, *noblesse oblige,* be magnificent, and as for the rest of the people, it did not matter much so long as they worked hard and stayed quiet.   There were upheavals, of course, and now and then a slave with a braver heart and a stouter spirit than his companions incited them to rebellion.   His head was chopped off for his pains and he was promptly forgotten.   The majority of the people for thousands of years honestly believed that this was the only orderly basis upon which society could be organized.

Nebulous ideas of a brotherhood, in which each man was to have an equal chance with every other, burned brightly for a little while in various parts of the world at different times, and flickered out. They broke forth with the fury of an explosion in France during the Revolution and in Russia during the Red Terror. They have smoldered quietly in some places and had just begun to break through with a steady, even flame. But America struck the match and gathered the wood to start her own fire. She is the first country in the world which was founded especially to promote individual freedom and the brotherhood of mankind. She had, to change the figure slightly, a blue-print to start with and she has been building ever since.

Her material came from the eastern hemisphere. The nations there at the time when the United States was settled were at different stages of their development. Some were vigorous with youth, some were in the height of their glory, and some were dying because the descendants of the men who had made them great were futile and incapable. These nations were different in race and religion, in thought, language, traditions, and temperament. When they were not quarreling with each other, they were busy with domestic squabbles. They had kept this up for centuries and were at it when the settlers landed at Jamestown and later when the *May-*

flower came to Plymouth Rock. Yet, with a cheerful disregard of the past and an almost sublime hope in the future they expected to live happily ever after they crossed the Atlantic Ocean. Needless to add, they did not.

Accident of place cannot change a man's color (though it may bleach it a shade lighter or tan it a shade darker), nor his religion nor any of the other racial and inherent qualities which are the result of slow centuries of development. And the same elements which made men fight in the old countries set them against each other in the new. Most of the antagonisms were and are the result of prejudices, foolish narrow prejudices, which, nevertheless, must be beaten down before we can expect genuine courtesy.

Further complications arose, and are still arising, from the fact that we did not all get here at the same time. Those who came first have inevitably and almost unconsciously formulated their own system of manners. Wherever there is community life and a certain amount of leisure there is a standard of cultivated behavior. And America, young as she is, has already accumulated traditions of her own.

It is beyond doubt that the men who came over in the early days were, as a rule, better timber than the ones who come now. They came to live and die, if necessary, for a religious or a political principle, for adventure, or like the debtors in Oglethorpe's colony in Georgia, to wipe clean the slate of the past and begin life again. To-day they come to make money or because they think they will find life easier here than it was where they were. And one of the chief reasons for the discontent and unrest (and, incidentally, rudeness) which prevails among them is that they find it hard. We are speaking in general terms. There are glorious exceptions.

The sturdy virtues of the pioneers did not include politeness. They never do. So long as there is an animal fear of existence man cannot think of minor elegances. He cannot live by bread alone, but he cannot live at all without it. Bread must come first. And the Pilgrim Father was too busy learning how to wring a living from the forbidding rocks of New England with one hand while he fought off the Indians with the other to give much time to tea parties and luncheons. Nowhere in America except in the South, where the leisurely life of the plantations gave opportunity for it, was any great attention paid to formal courtesy. But everywhere, as soon as the country had been tamed and prosperity began to peep over the horizon, the pioneers began to grow polite. They had time for it.

What we must remember—and this is a reason, not an excuse, for bad manners—is that these new people coming into the country, the present-day immigrants, are pioneers, and that the life is not an easy one whether it is lived among a wilderness of trees and beasts in a forest or a wilderness of men and buildings in a city. The average American brings a good many charges against the foreigner—some of them justified, for much of the "back-wash" of Europe and Asia has drifted into our harbor—but he must remember this: Whatever his opinion of the immigrant may be the fault is ours—he came into this country under the sanction of our laws. And he is entitled to fair and courteous treatment from every citizen who lives under the folds of the American flag.

The heterogeneous mixture which makes up our population is a serious obstacle (but not an insuperable one) in the way of courtesy, but there is another even greater. The first is America's problem. The second belongs to the world.

Material progress has raced so far ahead of mental and spiritual progress that the world itself is a good many years in advance of the people who are living in it. Our statesmen ride to Washington in automobiles and sleeping cars, but they are not vastly preferable to those who went there in stagecoaches and on horseback. In other words, there has been considerably more improvement in the vehicles which fill our highways than there has been in the people who ride in them.

The average man—who is, when all is said and done, the most important person in the state—has stood still while the currents of science and invention have swept past him. He has watched the work of the world pass into the keeping of machines, shining miracles of steel and electricity, and has forgot himself in worshipping them. Now he is beginning to realize that it is much easier to make a perfect machine than it is to find a perfect man to put behind it, and that man himself, even at his worst (and that is pretty bad) is worth more than anything else in the scheme of created things.

This tremendous change in environment resulting from the overwhelming domination of machinery has brought about a corresponding change in manners. For manners consist, in the main, of adapting oneself to one's surroundings. And the story of courtesy is the story of evolution.

It is interesting to run some of our conventions back to their origin. Nearly every one of them grew out of a practical desire for lessening friction or making life pleasanter.   The first gesture of courtesy was, no doubt, some form of greeting by which one man could know another as a friend and not an enemy.   They carried weapons then as habitually as they carry watches to-day and used them as frequently, so that when a man approached his neighbor to talk about the prospects of the sugar or berry crop he held out his right hand, which was the weapon hand, as a sign of peace.   This eventually became the handshake.   Raising one's hat is a relic of the days of chivalry when knights wore helmets which they removed when they came into the house, both because they were more comfortable without them and because it showed their respect for the ladies, whom it was their duty to serve.   And nearly every other ceremony which has lasted was based on common sense.   "Etiquette," as Dr. Brown has said, "with all its littlenesses and niceties, is founded upon a central idea of right and wrong."

The word "courtesy" itself did not come into the language until late (etiquette came even later) and then it was used to describe the polite practices at court.   It was wholly divorced from any idea of character, and the most fastidious gentlemen were sometimes the most complete scoundrels. Even the authors of books of etiquette were men of great superficial elegance whose moral standards were scandalously low. One of them, an Italian, was banished from court for having published an indecent poem and wrote his treatise on polite behavior while he was living in enforced retirement in his villa outside the city. It was translated for the edification of the young men of England and France and served as a standard for several generations. Another, an Englishman, spent the later years of his life writing letters to his illegitimate son, telling him exactly how to conduct himself in the courtly (and more or less corrupt) circles to which his noble rank entitled him. The letters were bound into a fat, dreary volume which still sits on the dust-covered shelves of many a library, and the name of the author has become a synonym for exquisite manners. Influential as he was in his own time, however, neither he nor any of the others of the early arbiters of elegance could set himself up as a dictator of what is polite to American men, of no matter what class, and get by with it. Not very far by, at any rate.

It is impossible now to separate courtesy and character. Politeness is a fundamental, not a superficial, thing. It is the golden rule translated into terms of conduct. It is not a whitewash which, if laid on thick enough, will cover every defect. It is a clear varnish which shows the texture and grain of the wood beneath. In the ideal democracy the ideal citizen is the man who is not only incapable of doing an ungallant or an ungracious thing, but is equally incapable of doing an unmanly one. There is no use lamenting the spacious days of long ago. Wishing for them will not bring them back. Our problem is to put the principles of courtesy into practice even in this hurried and hectic Twentieth Century of ours. And since the business man is in numbers, and perhaps in power also, the most consequential person in the country, it is of most importance that he should have a high standard of behavior, a high standard of civility, which includes not only courtesy but everything which has to do with good citizenship.

We have no desire for candy-box courtesy. It should be made of sterner stuff. Nor do we care for the sort which made the polite Frenchman say, "Excusez-moi" when he stabbed his adversary. We can scarcely hope just yet to attain to the magnificent calm which enabled Marie Antoinette to say, "I'm sorry. I did not do it on purpose," when she stepped on the foot of her executioner as they stood together on the scaffold, or Lord Chesterfield, gentleman to the very end, to say, "Give Dayrolles a chair" when his physician came into the room in which he lay dying. But we do want something that will enable us to live together in the world with a minimum degree of friction.

The best of us get on one another's nerves, even under ordinary conditions, and it takes infinite pains and self-control to get through a trying day in a busy office without striking sparks somewhere. If there is a secret of success, and some of the advertisements seem trying to persuade us that it is all secret, it is the ability to work efficiently and pleasantly with other people. The business man never works alone. He is caught in the clutches of civilization and there is no escape. He is like a man climbing a mountain tied to a lot of other men climbing the same mountain. What each one does affects all the others.

We do not want our people to devote themselves entirely to the art of being agreeable. If we could conceive of a world where everybody was perfectly polite and smiling all the time we should hardly like to live in it. It is human nature not to like perfection, and most of us, if brought face to face with that model of behavior, Mr. Turveydrop, who spent his life serving as a pattern of deportment, would sympathize with the delightful old lady who looked at him in the full flower of his glory and cried viciously (but under her breath) "I could bite you!"

When Pope Benedict XI sent a messenger to Giotto for a sample of his work the great artist drew a perfect circle with one sweep of his arm and gave it to the boy. Before his death Giotto executed many marvelous works of art, not one of them perfect, not even the magnificent bell tower at Florence, but all of them infinitely greater than the circle. It is better, whether one is working with bricks or souls, to build nobly than to build perfectly.

II

THE VALUE OF COURTESY

EVERY progressive business man will agree with the successful Western manufacturer who says that "courtesy can pay larger dividends in proportion to the effort expended than any other of the many human characteristics which might be classed as Instruments of Accomplishment." But this was not always true. In the beginning "big business" assumed an arrogant, high-handed attitude toward the public and rode rough-shod over its feelings and rights whenever possible. This was especially the case among the big monopolies and public service corporations, and much of the antagonism against the railroads to-day is the result of the methods they used when they first began to lay tracks and carry passengers. Nor was this sort of thing limited to the large concerns. Small business consisted many times of trickery executed according to David Harum's motto of "Do unto the other feller as he would like to do unto you, but do him fust." The public is a long-suffering body and the business man is a hard-headed one, but after a while the public began to realize that it was not necessary to put up with gross rudeness and the business man began to realize that a policy of pleasantness was much better than the "treat 'em rough" idea upon which he had been acting. He deserves no special credit for it. It was as simple and as obvious a thing as putting up an umbrella when it is raining.

People knew, long before this enlightened era of ours, that politeness had value. In one of the oldest books of good manners in the English language a man with "an eye to the main chance" advised his pupils to cultivate honesty, gentleness, propriety, and deportment because they paid. But it has not been until recently that business men as a whole have realized that courtesy is a practical asset to them. Business cannot be separated from money and there is no use to try. Men work that they may live. And the reason they have begun to develop and exploit courtesy is that they have discovered that it makes for better work and better living. Success, they have learned, in spite of the conspicuous wealth of several magnates who got their money by questionable means, depends upon good will and good will depends upon the square deal courteously given.

The time is within the memory of living men, and very young men at that, when the idea of putting courtesy into business dealings sprang up, but it has taken hold remarkably. When the Hudson Tubes were opened not quite a decade and a half ago Mr. McAdoo inaugurated what was at that time an almost revolutionary policy. He took the motto, "The Public be Pleased," instead of the one made famous by Mr. Vanderbilt, and posted it all about, had pamphlets distributed, and made a speech on courtesy in railroad management and elsewhere. Since that time, not altogether because of the precedent which had been established, but because people were beginning to realize that with this new element creeping into business the old régime had to die because it could not compete with it, there have been all sorts of courtesy campaigns among railroad and bus companies, and even among post office and banking employees, to mention only two of the groups .notorious for haughty and arrogant behavior. The effects of a big telephone company have been so strenuous and so well planned and executed that they are reserved for discussion in another chapter.

Mr. McAdoo tells a number of charming stories which grew out of the Hudson Tubes experiment. One day during a political convention when he was standing in the lobby of a hotel in a certain city a jeweler came over to him after a slight moment of hesitation, gave him one of his cards and said, "Mr. McAdoo, I owe you a great debt of gratitude. For that," he added, pointing to "The Public be Pleased" engraved in small letters on the card just above his name. "I was in New York the day the tunnel was opened," he continued, "and I heard your speech, and said to myself that it might be a pretty good idea to try that in the jewelry trade. And would you believe it, my profits during the first year were more than fifty per cent. bigger than they were the year before?" And we venture to add that the jeweler was more than twice as happy and that it was not altogether because there was more money in his coffers.

Mr. McAdoo is a man with whom courtesy is not merely a policy: it is a habit as well. He places it next to integrity of character as a qualification for a business man, and he carries it into every part of his personal activity, as the statesmen and elevator boys, waiters and financiers, politicians and stenographers with whom he has come into contact can testify. "I never have a secretary," he says, "who is not courteous, no matter what his other qualifications may be." During the past few years Mr. McAdoo has been placed in a position to be sought after by all kinds of people, and in nearly every instance he has given an interview to whoever has asked for it. "I have always felt," we quote him again, "that a public servant should be as accessible to the public as possible." Courtesy with him, as with any one else who makes it a habit, has a cumulative effect. The effect cannot always be traced as in the case of the jeweler or in the story given below in which money plays a very negligible part, but it is always there.

On one occasion—this was when he was president of the Hudson Railroad—Mr. McAdoo was on his way up to the Adirondacks when the train broke down. It was ill provided for such a catastrophe, there was no dining car, only a small buffet, and the wait was a long and trying one. When Mr. McAdoo after several hours went back to the buffet to see if he could get a cup of coffee and some rolls he found the conductor almost swamped by irate passengers who blamed him, in the way that passengers will, for something that was no more his fault than theirs. The conductor glanced up when Mr. McAdoo came in, expecting him to break into an explosion of indignation, but Mr. McAdoo said, "Well, you have troubles enough already without my adding to them."

The conductor stepped out of the group. "What did you want, sir?" he asked.

"Why, nothing, now," Mr. McAdoo responded. "I did want a cup of coffee, but never mind about it."

"Come into the smoker here," the conductor said. "Wait a minute."

The conductor disappeared and came back in a few minutes with coffee, bread, and butter. Mr. McAdoo thanked him warmly, gave him his card and told him that if he ever thought he could do anything for him to let him know. The conductor looked at the card.

"Are you the president of the Hudson Railroad?"

"Yes."

"Well, maybe there's something you can do for me now. There are two men out here who say they are going to report me for what happened this morning. You know how things have been, and if they do, I wish you would write to headquarters and explain. I'm in line for promotion and you know what a black mark means in a case like that."

Mr. McAdoo assured him that he would write if it became necessary. The men were bluffing, however, and the complaint was never sent in. Apparently the incident was closed.

Several years later Mr. McAdoo's son was coming down from the Adirondacks when he lost his Pullman ticket. He did not discover the fact until he got to the station, and then he had no money and no time to get any by wire before the train left. He went to the conductor, explained his dilemma, and told him that if he would allow him to ride down to the city his father, who was to meet him at the Grand Central station, would pay him for the ticket. The conductor liked the youngster—perhaps because there was something about him that reminded him of his father, for as chance would have it, the conductor was the same one who had brought Mr. McAdoo the coffee and bread in the smoking car so many months before.

"Who is your father?" he asked.

"Mr. McAdoo."

"President of the Hudson Railroad?"

"Yes."

"Boy, you can have the train!"

So far as monetary value of courtesy is concerned we might recount hundreds of instances where a single act of politeness brought in thousands of dollars. Only the other morning the papers carried the story of a man who thirty years ago went into a tailor's shop with a ragged tear in his trousers and begged the tailor to mend it and to trust him for the payment which amounted to fifty cents. The tailor agreed cheerfully enough and the man went his way, entered business and made a fortune. He died recently and left the tailor fifty thousand dollars. Not long before that there was a story of an old woman who came to New York to visit her nephew—it was to be a surprise—and lost her bearings so completely when she got into the station that she was about ready to turn around and go back home when a very polite young man noticed her bewilderment. He offered his services, called a taxi and deposited her in front of her nephew's door in half an hour. She took his name and address and a few days later he received a check large enough to enable him to enter the Columbia Law School. A banker is fond of telling the story of an old fellow who came into his bank one day in a suit of black so old that it had taken on a sickly greenish tinge. He fell into the hands of a polite clerk who answered all his questions—and there were a great many of them—clearly, patiently, and courteously. The old man went away but came back in a day or so with $300,000 which he placed on deposit. "I did have some doubts," he said, "but this young man settled them all." Word of it went to people in authority and the clerk was promoted.

Now it is pleasant to know that these good people were rewarded as they deserved to be. We would be very happy if we could promise a like reward to every one who is similarly kind, but it is no use. The little words of love and the little deeds of kindness go often without recompense so far as we can see, except that they happify the world, but that in itself is no small return.

Courtesy pays in dollars and cents but its value goes far beyond that. It is the chief element in building good will—we are speaking now of courtesy as an outgrowth of character— and good will is to a firm what honor is to a man. He can lose everything else but so long as he keeps his honor he has something to build with. In the same way a business can lose all its material assets and can replace them with insurance money or something else, but if it loses its good will it will find in ninety cases out of a hundred that it is gone forever and that the business itself has become so weakened that there is nothing left but to reorganize it completely and blot out the old institution altogether.

One must not make the mistake of believing that good will can be built on courtesy alone.

Courtesy must be backed up by something more solid. An excellent comparison to show the relation that good manners bear to uprightness and integrity of character was drawn a number of years ago by a famous Italian prelate. We shall paraphrase the quaint English of the original translator. "Just as men do commonly fear beasts that are cruel and wild," he says, "and have no manner of fear of little ones such as gnats and flies, and yet because of the continual nuisance which they find them, complain more of these than they do of the other: so most men hate the unmannerly and untaught as much as they do the wicked, and more. There is no doubt that he who wishes to live, not in solitary and desert places, like a hermit, but in fellowship with men, and in populous cities, will find it a very necessary thing, to have skill to put himself forth comely and seemly in his fashions, gestures, and manners: the lack of which do make other virtues lame."

Granting dependability of character, courtesy is the next finest business builder an organization can have. One of the largest trust companies in the world was built up on this hypothesis. A good many years ago the man who is responsible for its growth was cashier in a "busted" bank in a small city. The situation was a desperate one, for the bank could not do anything more for its customers than it was already doing. It could not give them more interest on their money and most of its other functions were mechanical. The young cashier began to wonder why people went to one bank in preference to another and in his own mind drew a comparison between the banking and the clothing business. He always went to the haberdasher who treated him best. Other men he knew did the same thing. Would not the same principle work in a bank? Would not people come to the place which gave them the best service? He decided to try it. Not only would they give efficient service, they would give it pleasantly. It was their last card but it was a trump. It won. The bank began to prosper. People who were annoyed by rude, brusque, or indifferent treatment in other banks came to this one. The cashier was raised to a position of importance and in an incredibly short time was made president of a trust company in New York. He carried with him exactly the same principle that had worked so well in the little bank and the result in the big one was exactly the same.

In a leaflet which is in circulation among the employees at this institution there are these paragraphs:

We ask you to remember:

That our customers *can* get along without us.

(There are in Greater New York nearly one hundred banks and trust companies, every one of them actively seeking business.)

We *cannot* get along without our customers.

A connection which, perhaps, it has taken us several months to establish, can be terminated by one careless or discourteous act.

Our customers are asked to maintain balances of certain proportions. If they wish to borrow money, they must deposit collateral. They must repay loans when they mature; or arrange for their extension.

If a bank errs, it must err on the side of safety, for the money it loans is not its own money but the money of its depositors. We (and every other bank and trust company) operate almost entirely on money which our customers have deposited with us. The least we can do, then, is to serve them courteously. They really are our employers.

Ours is a semi-public institution.

Every day, men try to interest us in matters with which we have no concern. It is our duty to tell these men, very courteously, why their proposals do not appeal to us. But they are entitled to a hearing. It may be that they are not in a position to benefit us, and never will be. But almost every man can harm us, if he tries to do so. And a pleasantly expressed declination invariably makes a better impression than a favor grudgingly granted. We ask you, then, to remember that our growth—and your opportunities—depend not only upon the friends we make, but *the enemies we do not make.*

Remember names and faces. Do something, say something that will bring home to those who do business with us the fact that the Blank Trust Company is a very human institution—that it wants the good will of every man and woman in the country.

That is the kind of courtesy which has builded this particular organization. It is a pleasure to visit it to-day because of the spirit of coöperation which animates it. They have done away with the elaborate spy systems in use in so many banks, although they keep the management well enough in hand to be able to fasten the blame for mistakes upon the right person. The employees work with one another and with the president, whom they adore. It is, as a matter of fact, largely the influence of the personality of the president filtering down through the ranks which has made possible the phenomenal success which the institution has enjoyed during the past few years, another proof of the fact that every institution—and Emerson was speaking of great institutions when he said it—"is the lengthened shadow of one man."

Banks have almost a peculiar problem. Money is a mighty power, and to the average person there is something very awesome about the place where it is kept. Mr. Stephen Leacock is not the only man who ever went into a bank with a funny little guilty feeling even when he had money in it.   When one is in this frame of mind it takes very little on the part of the clerk to make him believe that he has been treated rudely. Bank clerks are notoriously haughty, but the fault is often as much in the person on the outside as in the one on the inside of the bars, especially when he has come in to draw out money which he knows he should not, such as his savings bank account, for instance.   The other day a young man went into a savings bank to draw out all of his money for a purpose which he knew was extravagant although he had persuaded himself that it was not.   Throughout the whole time he was in the bank he was treated with perfect courtesy, but in spite of it he came out growling about "the dirty look the paying teller gave him!"

It is not only in the first contact that civility is important.   Eternal vigilance is the price of success as well as of liberty.   Another incident from the banking business illustrates this.   Several years ago a bank which had been steadily losing customers called in a publicity expert to build up trade for them.   The man organized a splendid campaign and things started off with a flourish.   People began to come in most gratifying numbers.   But they did not stay.   An investigation conducted by the publicity man disclosed the fact that they had been driven away by negligent and discourteous service.   He went to the president of the bank and told him that he was wasting money building up advertising so long as his bank maintained its present attitude toward the public.   The president was a man of practical sense.   There was a general clearing up, those who were past reform were discharged and those who stayed were given careful training in what good breeding meant and there was no more trouble.   Advertising will bring in a customer but it takes courtesy to keep him.

Business, like nearly everything else, is easier to tear down than to build up, and one of the most devastating instruments of destruction is discourtesy.   A contact which has taken years to build can be broken off by one snippy letter, one pert answer, or one discourteous response over the telephone.   Even collection letters, no matter how long overdue the accounts are, bring in more returns when they are written with tact and diplomacy than when these two qualities are omitted.   If you insult a man who owes you money he feels that the only way he can get even is not to pay you, and in most cases, he can justify himself for not doing it.

Within the organization itself a courteous attitude on the part of the men in positions of authority toward those beneath them is of immense importance.   Sap rises from the bottom, and a business has arrived at the point of stagnation when the men at the top refuse to listen to or help those around them.   It is, as a rule, however, not the veteran in commercial affairs but the fledgling who causes most trouble by his bad manners.   Young men, especially young men who have been fortunate in securing material advantages, too many times look upon the world as an accident placed here for their personal enjoyment.   It never takes long in business to relieve their minds of this delusion, but they sometimes accomplish a tremendous amount of damage before it happens.   For a pert, know-it-all manner coupled with the inefficiency which is almost inseparable from a total lack of experience is not likely to make personal contacts pleasant. Every young man worth his salt believes that he can reform the world, but every old man who has lived in it knows that it cannot be done.   Somewhere half way between they meet and say, "We'll keep working at it just the same," and then business begins to pick up.   But reaching the meeting ground takes tolerance and patience and infinite politeness from both sides.

"It is the grossest sort of incivility," the quotation is not exact, for we do not remember the source, "to be contemptuous of any kind of knowledge." And herein lies the difficulty between the hard-headed business man of twenty years' experience and the youngster upon whose diploma the ink has not yet dried. "Ignorance," declares a man who has spent his life in trying to draw capital and labor together and has succeeded in hundreds of factories, "is the cause of all trouble." And a lack of understanding, which is a form of ignorance, is the cause of nearly all discourtesy.

So long as there is discourtesy in the world there must be protection against it, and the best, cheapest, and easiest means of protection is courtesy itself. Boats which are in constant danger of being run into, such as the tug and ferry boats in a busy harbor, are fitted out with buffers or fenders which are as much a part of their equipment as the smokestack, and in many cases, as necessary. Ocean liners carry fenders to be thrown over the side when there is need for them, but this naturally is not as often as in more crowded waters. A single boat on a deserted sea with nothing but sea-gulls and flying fish in sight cannot damage any one besides herself. But the moment she enters a harbor she has to take into account every other vessel in it from the

Aquitania to the flat-bottomed row-boat with only one man in it. It is a remarkable fact that most of the boats that are injured or sunk by collision are damaged by vessels much smaller than themselves. Most of these accidents (this statement is given on the authority of an able seaman) could have been prevented by the use of a fender thrown over the side at the proper moment. Politeness is like this. It is the finest shock-absorber in the world, as essential from an economic point of view as it is pleasant from a social one. In business there is no royal isolation. We are all ferry boats. We need our shock absorbers every minute of the day.

No boat has a right to run into another, but they do it just the same, and a shock absorber is worth all the curses the captain and the crew can pronounce, however righteous their indignation toward the offending vessel. Sometimes politeness is better than justice.

Most of the causes of irritation during the course of a business day are too petty to bother about. Many of them could be ignored and a good many more could be laughed at. A sense of humor and a sense of proportion would do away with ninety per cent. of all the wrangling in the world. Some one has said, and not without truth, that a highly developed sense of humor

would have prevented the World War. Too
many people use sledge-hammers when tack
hammers would do just as well. They belong in
the same company with William Jay whose im-
mortal epitaph bears these words:

> Here lies the body of William Jay
> Who died maintaining his right of way.
> He was right, dead right, as he sped along,
> But he's just as dead as if he'd been wrong.

Courtesy is restful. A nervous frenzy of
energy throughout the day leaves one at sunset
as exhausted as a punctured balloon. The fussy
little fellow who fancies himself rushed to death,
who has no time to talk with anybody, who cannot be polite to his stenographer and his messenger boys because he is in such a terrible hurry, is
dissipating his energy into something that does
not matter and using up the vitality which should
go into his work. He is very like the engine
which President Lincoln was so fond of telling
about which used so much steam in blowing its
whistle that every time it did it it had to stop.

The Orientals manage things better than we
do. "We tried hurrying two thousand years
ago," a banker in Constantinople said to a tired
American business man, "and found that it did
not pay. So we gave it up." There is always

time to be polite, and though it sounds like a contradiction, there will be more time to spare if one devotes a part of his day to courtesy.

But there is danger in too much courtesy. Every virtue becomes a vice if it is carried too far, and frank rudeness is better than servility or hypocrisy. Commercial greed, there is no other name for it, leads a firm to adopt some such idiotic motto as "the customer is always right." No organization could ever live up to such a policy, and the principle back of it is undemocratic, un-American, unsound and untrue. The customer is not always right and the employer in a big (or little) concern who places girls (department stores are the chief sinners in this) on the front line of approach with any such instructions is a menace to self-respecting business. America does not want a serving class with a "king-can-do-no-wrong" attitude toward the public. Business is service, not servility, and courtesy works both ways. There is no more sense in business proclaiming that the customer is always right than there would be in a customer declaring that business is always right, and no more truth.

No good business man will argue with a customer, or anybody else, not only because it is bad policy to do so, but because his self-respect will

not allow it.   He will give and require from his
employees courteous treatment toward his customers, and when doubt arises he will give them
(the customers) the benefit of it.   And he will
always remember that he is dealing with an intelligent human being.   The customer has a
right to expect a firm to supply him with reliable
commodities and to do it pleasantly, but he has
no right to expect it to prostrate itself at his feet
in order to retain his trade, however large that
trade may be.

Too little has been said about courtesy on the
part of the customer and the public—that great
headless mass of unrelated particles.   Business
is service, we say, and the master is the public,
the hardest one in the world to serve.   Each one
of us speaks with more or less pitying contempt
of the public, forgetting that we ourselves are
the public and that the sum total of the good
breeding, intelligence, and character of the public can be no greater than that of the individuals
who make it up.

"Sid," of the *American Magazine,* says that
he once asked the manager of a circus which
group of his employees he had most trouble
keeping.   Quite unexpectedly the man replied,
"The attendants.   They get 'sucker-sore' and
after that they are no good."   This is how it

happens.   The wild man from Borneo is placed
in a cage with a placard attached bearing in big
letters the legend "The Wild Man from Borneo."   An old farmer comes to the circus, looks
at the wild man from Borneo in his cage, reads
the placard, looks at the attendant, "Is this the
wild man from Borneo?" he asks.   No human
being can stand an unlimited amount of this sort
of thing, and the attendant, after he has explained some hundred thousand or so times that
this really is the wild man from Borneo begins to
lose his zest for it and to answer snappishly and
sarcastically.   An infinite supply of courtesy
would, of course, be a priceless asset to him, but
does not this work both ways?   What right have
people to bother other people with perfectly foolish and imbecile questions?   Is there any one
who cannot sympathize with a "sucker-sore"
attendant?   And with the people who are stationed about for the purpose of answering questions almost anywhere?   There are not many of
us who at one time and another have not had the
feeling that we were on the wrong train even
after we had asked the man who sold us the
ticket, the man who punched it at the gate, the
guard who was standing near the entrance, and
the guard who was standing near the train, the
porter, the conductor, and the news-butcher if it

was the right one and have had an affirmative answer from every one of them.   How many times can a man be expected to answer such a question with a smile?   For those who are exposed to "suckers" the best advice is to be as gentle with them as possible, to grit your teeth and hold your temper even when the ninety-thousandth man comes through to ask if this is the right train. For the "suckers" themselves there are only two words of advice.   They include all the rest: Stop it.

It is impossible to tell what the value of courtesy is.   Perhaps some day the people who have learned to measure our minds will be able to tell us just what a smile is worth.   Maybe they can tell us also what Spring is worth, and what happiness is worth.   Meanwhile we do not know. We only know that they are infinitely precious.

III

PUTTING COURTESY INTO BUSINESS

WE TALK a great deal about gentlemen and about democracy and a good many other words which describe noble conceptions without a very clear idea of what they mean. The biggest mistake we make is in thinking of them as something stationary like a monument carved in granite or a stone set upon a hill, when the truth is that they are living ideas subject to the change and growth of all living things. No man has ever yet become a perfect gentleman because as his mind has developed his conception of what a gentleman is has enlarged, just as no country has ever become a perfect democracy because each new idea of freedom has led to broader ideas of freedom. It is very much like walking through a tunnel. At first there is only darkness, and then a tiny pin point of light ahead which grows wider and wider as one advances toward it until, finally, he stands out in the open with the world before him.   There is no end to life, and none to human development, at least none that can be conceived of by the finite mind of man.

There are hundreds of definitions of a gentleman, none of them altogether satisfactory. Cardinal Newman says it is almost enough to say that he is one who never gives pain. "They be the men," runs an old chronicle, "whom their race and bloud, or at the least, their virtues, do make noble and knowne." Barrow declares that they are the men lifted above the vulgar crowd by two qualities: courage and courtesy. The Century Dictionary, which is as good an authority as any, says, "A gentleman is a man of good breeding, courtesy, and kindness; hence, a man distinguished for fine sense of honor, strict regard for his obligations, and consideration for the rights and feelings of others." And this is a good enough working standard for anybody. The Dictionary is careful to make—and this is important—a gentleman not one who conforms to an outward and conventional standard, but one who follows an inward and personal ideal.

Of late days there has been a great deal of attention paid to making gentlemen of business men and putting courtesy into all the ramifications of business. Without doubt the chief reason for it is the fact that business men themselves have discovered that it pays.   One restaurant frankly adopted the motto, "Courtesy Pays," and had it all fixed up with gilt letters and framed and hung it near the front door, and a number of other places have exactly the same policy for exactly the same reason though they do not all proclaim the fact so boldly.   It is not the loftiest motive in the world but it is an intelligent one, and it is better for a man to be polite because he hopes to win success that way than for him not to be polite at all.

Human conduct, even at its best, is not always inspired by the highest possible motives.   Not even the religions which men have followed have been able to accomplish this.   Most of them have held out the hope of heavenly reward in payment for goodness here on earth and countless millions of men (and women, too, for that matter) have kept in the straight and narrow path because they were afraid to step out of it.   It may be that they were, intrinsically, no better men than the ones who trod the primrose path to the everlasting bonfire, but they were much easier to live with.   And the man who is courteous, who is a gentleman, whatever his motives, is a more agreeable citizen than the one who is not.

Now how—this is our problem—does one go

about making a gentleman? Environment plays, comparatively speaking, a very small part. "The appellation of gentleman," this is from a gentleman of the Seventeenth Century, "is not to be affixed to a man's circumstances, but to his behavior in them." It is extremely doubtful if courtesy can be taught by rule. It is more a matter of atmosphere, and an instinct "for the better side of things and the cleaner surfaces of life." And yet, heredity, training, and environment all enter into the process.

It is a polite and pleasant fiction that courtesy is innate and not acquired, and we hear a great deal about the "born lady" and the "born gentleman." They are both myths. Babies are not polite, and the "king upon 'is throne with 'is crown upon 'is 'ead" has had, if he is a gentleman, lifelong training in the art of being one. There is still in existence a very interesting outline which was given by Queen Victoria and Prince Albert to their oldest son, the Prince of Wales, on his seventeenth birthday. It contained a careful summary of what was expected of him as a Christian gentleman and included such items as dress, appearance, deportment, relations with other people, and ability to acquit himself well in whatever company he happened to be thrown.

The King and Queen, although they were probably unaware of the fact, were acting upon the advice of an authority on good manners at court a number of years before their time. "Indeed," says the old manuscript, "from seven to seventeen young gentlemen commonly are carefully enough brought up: but from seventeen to seven-and-twenty (the most dangerous time of all a man's life, and the most slippery to stay well in) they have commonly the rein of all license in their own hand, and specially such as do live in the court." If we bring the sentence up to date, and it is as true now as it was then, we may substitute "business" for "court." Business men as well as courtiers find the ages between seventeen and seven-and-twenty "the most slippery to stay well in" for it is during these years that they are establishing themselves in the commercial world. As a general thing, but it is wise to remember that there is no rule to which there are not exceptions, by the time a man is twenty-seven his habits are formed and it is too late to acquire new ones.

Most children undergo a painstaking and more or less painful course of instruction in good manners and know by the time they are men and women what should be done whether they do it or not. Our social code is not a complicated

one, and there is no excuse except for the youngsters who have just growed up like Topsy or
have been brought up by jerks like Pip.   It is,
without doubt, easier to be polite among people
who are naturally courteous than among those
who snap and snarl at one another, but it is a
mistake to place too much emphasis on this part
of it.   Too many men—business men, at that—
have come up out of the mire for us to be able to
offer elaborate apologies for those who have
stayed in it.   The background is of minor importance.   A cockroach is a cockroach anywhere
you put him.

It is easy to envy the men who have had superior advantages, and many a man feels that if
he had another's chance he, too, might have become a great gentleman.   It is an idle specula-
tion.   His own opportunities are the only ones
any man can attend to, and if he is sensible he
will take quick advantage of those that come, not
in dreams, but in reality, and will remember what
a very sagacious English statesman said about
matters of even graver import: "It makes no difference where you are going.   You've got to
start from where you are."

The lack of early training is a handicap but
not a formidable one, especially to a business
man.   As the Spaniards say, there is little curi-

osity about the pedigree of a good man. And
no man needs to be ashamed of his origin. The
president of a firm would naturally be interested
in the ancestry of a young man who came to ask
him for the hand of his daughter, but if the man
has come to sell a bill of goods he does not care a
snap. In discussions of the social evil it is often
said that every child has a right to be well born,
but Robert Louis Stevenson saw more deeply
and spoke more truly when he said, "We are all
nobly born; fortunate those who know it; blessed
those who remember."

The finest Gentleman the world has ever seen
was born some two thousand years ago to the
wife of a carpenter in Bethlehem and spent most
of His time among fishermen, tax-collectors,
cripples, lepers, and outcasts of various sorts;
and yet in the entire record of His short and
troubled life there is not one mention of an un-
graceful or an ungainly action. He was careful to observe even the trivialities of social life.
Mary and Martha were quarreling before dinner. He quieted them with a few gracious
words. The people at the marriage feast at
Cana were worried because they had only water
to drink. He touched it and gave them wine.
The multitude who came to hear Him were tired,
footsore, and hungry. He asked them to be

seated and gave them food.   He dined with the
Pharisees, He talked with the women of Sama-
ria, He comforted Mary Magdalen, and He
washed the feet of His disciples.   He was beset
and harassed by a thousand rude and unmannerly questions, but not once did He return an
impatient answer.   Surely these things are god-
like and divine whatever one may believe about
the relation of Jesus Christ to God, the Father.

It has been said that every man should choose
a gentleman for his father.   He should also
choose a gentleman for his employer.   Unfortunately he often has no more option in the one
than he has in the other.   Very few of us get exactly what we want.   But however this may be,
a gentleman at the head of a concern is a priceless asset.   The atmosphere of most business
houses is determined by the man at the top.   His
character filters down through the ranks.   If he
is a rough-and-tumble sort of person the office is
likely to be that kind of place; if he is quiet and
mannerly the chances are that the office will be
quiet and mannerly.   If he is a gentleman everybody in the place will know it and will feel the
effects of it.   "I am always glad John was with
Mr. Blank his first year in business," said a
mother speaking of her son.   Mr. Blank was a
man who had a life-long reputation for being as

straight as a shingle and as clean as a hound's tooth, every inch a gentleman.

"How do you account for the fact that you have come to place so much emphasis on courtesy?" a business man was asked one day as he sat in his upholstered office with great windows opening out on the New York harbor. He thought for a moment, and his mind went back to the little Georgia village where he was born and brought up. "My father was a gentleman," he answered. "I remember when I was a boy he used to be careful about such trifles as this. 'Now, Jim,' he would say, 'when you stop on the sidewalk don't stop in the middle of it. Stand aside so you won't be in anybody's way.' And even now," the man smiled, "I never stop on the sidewalk without stepping to one side so as to be out of the way."

The life of a young person is plastic, easy to take impressions, strong to retain them. And the "old man" or the "governor," whether he is father, friend, or employer, or all three, has infinitely more influence than either he or the young man realizes. At the same time it is perfectly true that young people do not believe what older ones tell them about life. They have to try it out for themselves. One generation does not begin where the other left off. Each one of us begins at the beginning, and the world, with all that it holds, is as wonderful (though slightly different, to be sure) and as new to the child who is born into it to-day as it was to Adam on the first morning after it was created.

It is almost tragic that so many young men take the tenor of their lives from that of their employers, especially if the latter have been successful. This places a terrific responsibility upon the employer which does not, however, shift it from the employee. His part in business or in life—and this is true of all of us—is what he makes it, great or small. And the most important thing is for him to have a personal ideal of what he thinks best and hold to it. He cannot get it from the outside.

"Courtesy is not one of the company's rules," wrote the manager of a large organization which has been very successful in handling men and making money. "It is a tradition, an instinct. It is an attribute of the general tone, of the dominating influence of the management in all its relations. It is a part of the general tone, the honor, the integrity of the company. For three generations it has been looked upon as an inheritance to be preserved and kept irreproachable. Employees are drawn into this influence by the very simple process of their own development. Those who find themselves in harmony with the character of the company or who deliberately put themselves in tune progress. Those who do not, cannot, for long, do congenial or acceptable service." This is the statement from the manager of a firm that is widely known for courteous dealing. Their standard is now established. It is a part of the atmosphere, and their chief problem is to get men who will fit into it.

An employer does not judge a man on an abstract basis. He takes him because he thinks he will be useful to his business. This is why most places like to get men when they are young. They are easier to train.

Every one likes good material to work with, and employers are no exception. They take the best they can find, and the higher the standard of the firm the greater the care expended in choosing the employees. "Whenever we find a good man," said the manager of a big trust company, "we take him on. We may not have a place for him at the time but we keep him until we find one."

Except during times of stress such as that brought about by the war when the soldiers were at the front, no business house hires people indiscriminately.   They know, as the Chinese have it, that rotten wood cannot be carved.   "It is our opinion," we quote from another manager, "that courtesy cannot be pounded into a person who lacks proper social basis.   In other words, there are some people who would be boorish under any circumstances.   Our first and chief step toward courtesy is to exercise care in selecting our employees.   We weigh carefully each applicant for a sales position and try to visualize his probable deportment as our representative, and unless he gives promise of being a fit representative we do not employ him."

But it is not enough to take a man into a business organization.   Every newcomer must be broken in.   Sometimes this is done by means of formal training, sometimes it consists merely of giving him an idea of what is expected of him and letting him work out his own salvation. Granting that he is already familiar with the work in a general way, and that he is intelligent and resourceful, he ought to be able to adapt himself without a great deal of instruction from above.   All of this depends upon the kind of work which is to be done.

Nearly every employer exercises more caution in selecting the man who is to meet the public than any other. It is through him that the all-important first impression is made, and a man who is rude or discourteous, or who, for any reason, rubs people the wrong way, simply will not do. He may have many virtues but unless they are apparent they are for the time being of little service.

Most salesmen have to go to school. Their work consists largely of the study of one of the most difficult subjects in the catalogue: human psychology. They must know why men do what they do and how to make them do what they, the salesmen, want them to do. They must be able to handle the most delicate situations courteously and without friction. It takes the tact of a diplomat, the nerve of a trapeze performer, the physical strength of a prize fighter, the optimism of William J. Bryan or of Pollyanna, and the wisdom of Solomon. Not many men are born with this combination of qualities.

The best training schools base their teaching on character and common sense. One very remarkable organization, which has at its head an astonishingly buoyant and optimistic—and, it is hardly necessary to add, successful—man, teaches that character is nine-tenths of success in salesmanship and technique is only one-tenth. They study technique and character along with it, in a scientific way, like the students in a biological laboratory who examine specimens.   Their prospects are their subjects, and while they do not actually bring them into the consultation room, they hold experience meetings and tell the stories of their successful and unsuccessful contacts.   The meetings are held at the end of the day, when the men are all tired and many of them are depressed and discouraged. They are opened with songs, "My Old Kentucky Home," "Old Black Joe," "Sweet Adeline," and the other good old familiar favorites that make one think of home and mother and school days and happiness.   One or two catchy popular songs are introduced, and the men sing or hum or whistle or divide into groups and do all three with all their might.   It is irresistible.   Fifteen or twenty minutes of it can wipe out the sourest memory of the day's business, and trivial irritations sink to their proper place in the scheme of things.   The little speeches follow, and the men clap and cheer for the ones who have done good work and try to make an intelligent diagnosis of the cases of the ones who have not.   When the leader talks he sometimes recounts his early experiences—he, like most good salesmanagers, was once on the road himself—and if he is in an inspirational mood, gives a sound talk on the principle back of the golden rule. The spirit of coöperation throughout the institution is amazing and the morale is something any group of workers might well envy them.

Most business houses recognize their responsibilities toward the young people that they hire. Well-organized concerns build up from within. The heads of the departments are for the most part men who have received their training in the institution, and they take as much pains in selecting their office boys as they do in selecting any other group, for it is in them that they see the future heads and assistant heads of the departments. In hiring office boys "cleanness, good manners, good physique, mental agility, and good habits are primary requisites," according to Mr. J. Ogden Armour in the *American Magazine*.

In one of the oldest banks in New York each boy who enters is given a few days' intensive training by a gentleman chosen for the purpose. The instructor stresses the fundamentals of character and, above all things, common sense. Courtesy is rarely discussed as a separate quality but simple instructions are given about not going in front of a person when there is room to go around him, not pushing into an elevator ahead of every one else, not speaking to a man at a desk until he has signified that he is ready, and about sustaining quiet and orderly behavior everywhere. The atmosphere in the bank is the kind that encourages gentlemanly conduct and the new boys either fall in with it or else get out and go somewhere else.

It takes more patience on the part of the youngsters in the financial district than it does in most other places, for the men there work under high tension and are often cross, worried, nervous, and irritable, and as a result are, many times, without intending it, unjust. The discipline is severe, and the boy would not be human if he did not resent it. But the youngster who is quick to fly off the handle will find himself sadly handicapped, however brilliant he may be, in the race with boys who can keep their tempers in the face of an injury.

Three boys out of the hundreds who have passed through the training school in the bank of which we were speaking have been discharged for acts of discourtesy. One flipped a rubber clip across a platform and hit one of the officials in the eye, one refused to stay after hours to finish some work he had neglected during the day, and one was impertinent. All three could have stayed if each had used a little common sense, and all three could have stayed if each act had not been a fair indication of his general attitude toward his work.

One of the most difficult organizations to manage and one against which the charge of discourtesy is frequently brought is the department store. Yet a distinguished Englishwoman visiting here—it takes a woman to judge these things—said, "I had always been told that people in New York were in such a hurry that, although well-meaning enough, they were inclined to appear somewhat rude to strangers. I have found it to be just the reverse. During my first strolls in the streets, in the shops, and elsewhere, I have found everybody most courteous. Your stores, I may say, are the finest I have ever seen, not excepting those of Paris. Their displays are remarkable. Their spaciousness impressed me greatly. Even at a crowded time it was not difficult to move about. In London, where our shops are mostly cramped and old-fashioned, it would be impossible for such large numbers of people to find admittance."

The tribute is a very nice one. For a long time the department stores have realized the difficulties under which they labor and have been making efforts to overcome them. They have formed associations by which they study each other's methods, and most of them have very highly organized systems of training and management. One big department store carries on courtesy drives. Talks are given, posters are exhibited, and prizes are offered for the most courteous clerks in the store. "We know that it is not fair to give prizes," the personnel manager says, "because it is impossible to tell really which clerks are the most courteous, but it stimulates interest and effort throughout the organization and the effects last after the drive is over."

One big department store which is favorably known among a large clientele for courteous handling of customers depends upon its atmosphere to an enormous extent, but it realizes that atmosphere does not come by chance, that it has to be created. They have arranged it so that each clerk has time to serve each customer who enters without the nervous hurry which is the cause of so much rudeness. The salesclerks who come into the institution are given two weeks' training in the mechanical end of their work, the ways of recording sales, methods of approach, and so on, as well as in the spirit of coöperation and service. By the time the clerk is placed behind the counter he or she can conduct a sale courteously and with despatch, but there is never a time when the head of the department is not ready and willing to be consulted about extraordinary situations which may arise.

It is during the rush seasons such as the three or four weeks which precede Christmas that courtesy is put to the severest test, and the store described in the paragraph above bears up under it nobly. It did not wait until Christmas to begin teaching courtesy. It had tried to make it a habit, but last year several weeks before the holidays it issued a bulletin to its employees to remind them of certain things that would make the Christmas shopping less nerve-racking. The first paragraph was headed HEALTH. It ran as follows:

"If you want to be really merry at Christmas time, it will be well to bear in mind during this busy month at least these few 'health savers':

"Every night try to get eight good hours of sleep.

"All day try to keep an even temper and a ready smile.

"Remember that five minutes lost in the morning means additional pressure all day long.

"Try to make your extra effort a steady one— not allowing yourself to get excited and rushed so that you make careless mistakes.

"Try to eat regularly three good nourishing

meals, relaxing completely while you are at the table and for a little while afterward.

"Breathe deeply, and as often as you can, good fresh air—it cures weariness.

"And don't forget that a brisk walk, a sensible dinner, an hour's relaxation, and then a hot bath before retiring, make a refreshing end for one business day and a splendid preparation for the next."

There were six other paragraphs in the bulletin. One asked the salesclerks to take the greatest care in complying with a customer's request to send gift purchases without the price tags. Another asked them to pay strictest attention to getting the right addresses, and most of the others were taken up with suggestions for ways to avoid congestion by using a bank of elevators somewhat less conveniently located than the others, by limiting their personal telephone calls to those which were absolutely necessary, and so on. In both tone and content the bulletin was an excellent one. It first considered the employees and then the customers. There was no condescension in the way it was written and there was no "bunk" about what was in it. But the bulletin was only a small part of an effort that never stops.

The purpose of the store is, to quote from its

own statement, "to render honest, prompt, courteous and complete service to customers" and the qualities by which they measure their employees are as follows:

Health	Accuracy
Loyalty	Thoroughness
Coöperation	
Initiative	Responsibility
Industry	Knowledge

Courtesy is not included in the list but it is unnecessary. If these qualities are developed courtesy will come of its own accord. It is worth noting that health comes first in the list. To a business man, or indeed to any other, it is one of the most precious possessions in the world, and is the best of backgrounds upon which to embroider the flower of courtesy.

Every employer who has had any experience knows the value of a contented workman, and does what he can to make and keep him so by paying him adequate wages, and providing comfortable, sanitary, and pleasant working conditions. Contentment is, however, more an attitude of mind than a result of external circumstances. Happiness is who, not where, you are. We do not mean by this that a workman should be wholly satisfied and without ambition or that he should face the world with a permanent grin, but that he should to the best of his ability follow that wonderful motto of Roosevelt's, "Do what you can where you are with what you have." No man can control circumstances; not even the braggart Napoleon, who declared that he made circumstances, could control them to the end; and no man can shape them to suit exactly his own purposes, but every man can meet them bravely as a gentleman should.

Most big business concerns supply rest rooms, eating places, recreation camps, and all manner of comforts for their employees, and most of them maintain welfare departments. No business house under heaven could take the place of a home, but where the home influence is bad the best counterfoil is a wholesome atmosphere in which to work. Recently an institution advertising for help, instead of asking what the applicant could do for it, pictured and described what it could do for the applicant. The result was that they got a high-class group of people to make their selection from, and their attitude was one which invited the newcomers to do their best.

Factory owners are paying a good deal of attention to the appearance of their buildings. Many of them have moved out into the country so as to provide more healthful surroundings for work.   Numbers of modern factory buildings are very beautiful to look at, trim white buildings set in close-cut lawns with tennis courts and swimming pools not far away, red brick buildings covered with ivy, sand-colored ones with roses climbing over them, and others like the one famous for its thousand windows, rather more comfortable than lovely.   In our big cities there are office buildings that look like cathedrals, railroad stations that look like temples, and traffic bridges that look (from a distance) like fairy arches leading into the land of dreams.   They are not all like this.   We wish they were.   But it is to the credit of the American business man that he has put at least a part of his life and work into the building of beautiful things.   The influence which comes from them is, like nearly all potent influences, an unconscious one, but it makes for happiness and contentment.

The problem of keeping the employees contented is somewhat different in every place. House organs, picnics, dances, recreation parks, sanitariums in the country and so on can be utilized by "big business," but the spirit which animates them is the same as that which makes the grocery man at Hicksville Centre give his delivery boy an afternoon off when the baseball team comes to town. The spirit of courtesy is everywhere the same, but it must be kept in mind that the end of business is production, production takes work, and that play is introduced in order that the work may be better. This is true whether we are looking at the matter from the point of view of the employer or of the employee. What is to the interest of one—this is gaining slow but sure recognition—is to the interest of the other.

Certain kinds of mechanical work are very trying because of their monotony. The work must be done, however, and in well-ordered places it is arranged so that the worker has brief periods of rest at regular intervals or so that he is shifted from one kind of activity to another. It is poor economy to wear out men. In the old days before the power of steam or electricity had been discovered, boats were propelled by slaves who were kept below decks chained to their seats, and watched by an overseer who forced them to continue rowing long after they had reached the point of exhaustion. The galley slave sat always on the same side of the boat and after a few years his body became so twisted and warped that he was no good for anything else, and pretty soon was not even good for that. Then he was thrown into the discard—most of them died before they got this far along—and the owner of the boat had to look out for more men.   Something like this happens to the soul of a man who is bound to dreary, monotonous work without relief or any outlet for growth.   It is deadening to him, to his work, and to his employer.   The far-sighted employer knows it.   The masters of slaves learned it many years ago.   The chain which binds the servant to the master binds the master to the servant.   And the fastening is as secure at one end as it is at the other.

Too strict supervision—slave-driving—is fatal to courtesy.   The places which have intricate spy systems to watch their employees are the ones where there is most rudeness and trickery.   The clerk who is hectored, nagged, spied upon, suspected and scolded by some hireling brought in for that purpose or by the head of the firm himself cannot be expected to give "a smile with every purchase and a thank you for every good-bye."   The training of employees never stops, but it is something that should be placed very largely in their own hands. After a certain point supervision should be unnecessary.

Most places hate to discharge a man.   Labor turnover is too expensive.   Most of them try to place their men in the positions for which they are best suited.   It is easier to take a round peg out of a square hole and put it into a round one than it is to send out for another assortment of pegs. Men are transferred from sales departments to accounting departments, are taken off the road and brought into the home office, and are shifted about in various ways until they fit. If a man shows that "he has it in him" he is given every chance to succeed. "There is only one thing we drop a man for right off," says an employment manager in a place which has in its service several thousand people of both sexes, "and that is for saying something out of the way to one of our girls."

This same manager tells the story of a boy he hired and put into a department which had been so badly managed that there were a number of loose ends to be tied up. The boy threw himself into his work, cleared up things, and found himself in a "soft snap" without a great deal to do. He happened not to be the kind of person who can be satisfied with a soft snap, and he became so restive and unhappy that he was recommended for discharge. This brought him back to the head of the employment bureau. He, instead of throwing the young man out, asked that he be given a second trial in a department where the loose ends could not be cleaned up. It was a place where there was always plenty of work to do, and the young man has been happy and has been doing satisfactory work ever since.

The house in which this happened is always generous toward the mistakes of its employees if the mistakes do not occur too persistently and too frequently. In one instance a boy made three successive errors in figures in as many days. He was slated for discharge but sent first before the employment manager. As they talked the latter noticed that the boy leaned forward with a strained expression on his face. Thinking perhaps he was slightly deaf, he lowered his voice, but the boy understood every word he said. Then he noticed that there was a tiny red ridge across his nose as if he were accustomed to wearing glasses, although he did not have them on, and when he asked about it he discovered that the boy had broken his glasses a few days before, and that he had not had them fixed because he did not have money enough.

"Why didn't you tell us about it?" the employment manager asked.

"It was not your fault that I broke them," the boy replied. "It was up to me," an independent answer which in itself indicates how much worth while it was to keep him.

The manager gave him money enough to have

the glasses mended, the next day the boy was back at work, and there was no more trouble.

An employee in the same organization unintentionally did something which hurt the president of the firm a great deal. But when he went to him and apologized (it takes a man to admit that he is wrong and apologize for it) the president sent him back to his desk, "It's all right, boy," he said, "I know you care. That's enough."

In a big department store in New England there was a girl a few years back with an alert mind, an assertive personality, and a tremendous fund of energy. She was in the habit of giving constructive suggestions to the heads of the departments in which she worked, and because of her youth and manner, they resented it. "I took her into my office," the manager said. "I'm the only one she can be impertinent to there and I don't mind it. It is a bad manifestation of a good quality, and in time the disagreeable part of it will wear off. She will make an excellent business woman."

"If a man finds fault with a boy without explaining the cause to him," we are quoting here from an executive in a highly successful Middle Western firm, "I won't fire the boy, I fire the man. We have not a square inch of space in this organization for the man who criticizes a subordinate without telling him how to do better." Unless the plan of management is big enough to include every one from the oldest saint to the youngest sinner it is no good. Business built on oppression and cut-throat competition, whether the competition is between employer and employee or between rival firms, is war, and war, industrial or political, is still what General Sherman called it some years ago.

We hold no brief for paternalism. We have no patience with it. All that we want is a spirit of fairness and coöperation which will give every man a chance to make good on his own account. This spirit inevitably flowers into courtesy. In every place courtesy should be, of course, so thoroughly a part of the surroundings that it is accepted like air or sunshine without comment. But it is not, and never has been except in old civilizations where manners have ripened and mellowed under the beneficent influence of time. Our traditions here—speaking of the country as a whole—are still in the making, but we have at least got far enough along to realize that it is not only worth while to do things that are good, but, as an old author has it, to do them with a good grace. It cannot be accomplished overnight. Courtesy is not like a fungous growth springing up in a few hours in the decayed parts of a tree; it is like that within the tree itself which gives lustre to the leaves and a beautiful surface to the whole.   It takes time to develop it—time and patience—but it is worth waiting for.

IV

PERSONALITY

ALL that makes a man who he is and not someone else is called personality. It is the sum total of his qualities, a thing inborn, but including besides such externals as dress, manner, and appearance. It is either a tremendous asset or a terrific liability, and so important that certain schools which purport to teach success in business declare that it is everything. Which is just as foolish as saying that it is nothing.

One of these success-before-you-wake-to-morrow-morning schools of business instruction dismisses the fact which has remained true through three thousand years of change, namely, that there is no short cut to success, as a myth, and even goes so far as to say that it is almost impossible to achieve success to-day by working for it. E. H. Harriman they give as an example of a man who did no work but won success by smoking cigars while other men built railroads for him, quoting a joking remark of his to prove a serious point, when, as a matter of fact, Mr. Harriman was one of the large number of American business men who have literally worked themselves to death. Foch said that he won the war by smoking his pipe, but does any one believe that the great commander won the war by not working? What he meant was that he won the war by thinking, and the worn face, which seemed almost twice as old when the conflict was over, showed how hard that work was.

It is so impossible for a false doctrine to stand on its own feet that the spread-eagle advertisement of this school contradicts itself long before it gets to the "Sign here and mail to-day" coupon. "The first time you try to swim," shouts the advertisement, "for instance, you sink; and the first time you try to ride a bicycle you fall off. But the ability to do these things was born in you. And shortly you can both swim and ride. Then you wonder why you could not always do these things. They seem so absurdly simple." It may be that there are people who have learned to swim and to ride a bicycle by sitting in a chair and cultivating certain inherent qualities but we have never heard of them. Everybody that we ever knew worked and worked hard swimming and riding before they learned. The only way to learn to do a job is to do it, and the only way to succeed is to work. Any school or any person who says that "the most important thing for you to do is not to work, but first to find the short road to success. After that you may safely work all you like—but as a matter of fact, you won't have to work very hard," is a liar and a menace to the country and to business.

But the value of personality is not to be underestimated. "Nature," says Thackeray somewhere in "The Virginians," "has written a letter of credit upon some men's faces, which is honored almost wherever presented. Harry Warrington's [Harry Warrington was the hero who brought about this observation] countenance was so stamped in his youth. His eyes were so bright, his cheeks so red and healthy, his look so frank and open, that almost all who beheld him, nay, even those who cheated him, trusted him." It was the "letter of credit" stamped upon the face of Roosevelt, pledge of the character which lay behind it, which made him the idol of the American people.

Personality is hard to analyze and harder still to acquire. The usual advice given to one who is trying to cultivate a pleasing manner and address is "Be natural," but this cannot be taken too literally. Most of us find it perfectly natural to be cross and disagreeable under trying circumstances. It would be natural for a man to cry out profane words when a woman grinds down on his corn but it would not be polite. It was natural for Uriah Heep to wriggle like an eel, but that did not make it any the less detestable. It was natural, considering the past history of Germany and the system under which he was educated, for the Kaiser to want to be lord of the world, but that did not make it any the less horrible.

Another bromidic piece of advice is "Be perfectly frank and sincere." But this, too, has its limits. Some people pride themselves on saying exactly what they think. Usually they are brutal, insensitive, wholly incapable of sympathetic understanding of any one else, and cursed, besides, with a colossal vanity. A man may determine to tell nothing but the truth, but this does not make it necessary for him to tell the whole truth, especially when it will hurt the feelings or the reputation of some one else. No man has a right to impose his opinions and prejudices, his sufferings and agonies, on other people. It is the part of a coward to whine.

And yet a man must be himself, must be natural and sincere. Roosevelt could no more have adopted the academic manner of Wilson than Wilson could have adopted the boyish manner of Roosevelt. Lincoln could no more have adopted the courtly grace of Washington than Washington could have adopted the rugged simplicity of Lincoln. Nor would such transformations be desirable even if they were possible. The world would be a very dreary place if we were all cut by the same pattern.

A number of years ago in an upstate town in New York there was a shoe store which had been built up by the engaging personality of the man who owned it. He had worked his way up from a tiny shoe shop in New Jersey where, as a boy, he made shoes by hand before there were factories for the purpose, and he had always kept in close touch with the business even after he owned a large establishment and had a number of men working under him. He stayed in the shop, greeted his customers as they came in, and many times waited on them himself.

When he retired from active business he sold out to a man exactly his opposite in temperament, as good a man, so far as character went, as himself, but very quiet and taciturn. A woman who had always patronized the shop and was a friend of them both came to him soon after the transfer was made and said, "Now, Mr. Tillis, the reason this place has prospered so is on account of the personality of Mr. Kilbourne.

His shoes are good but people can get good shoes at other places. They come here because of Mr. Kilbourne. They like him, and if you are not careful they will stop coming now that he is gone. You've got to smile and show them you are glad to see them."

Mr. Tillis felt that the woman was telling the truth. He decided that he would stay in the shop and greet each customer with a gladsome smile and make himself generally pleasant and agreeable. The next day he was fitting a shoe on a woman who was also an old customer and a friend of both men. He was smiling in his best manner and congratulating himself that he was doing very well when the woman abruptly took her foot off the stand. "What are you laughing at?" she demanded.

Some years later he told Mr. Kilbourne about it. "I decided then that there was no use in me trying to be you. You had been yourself, and I made up my mind that I'd be myself."

And that is, after all, the only rule that can be given. Be yourself, but be very sure that it is your best self.

It is personality which permits one man to do a thing that another would be shot for. What is charming in this man is disgusting in that. What is a smile with one becomes a smirk with another. What makes one succeed will cause another to fail. It is personality that opens the doors of opportunity. It cannot, alone, keep them open, but it is worth a good deal to get inside.

We were interested to observe the methods used by three young men who were looking for jobs, not one of whom would probably have succeeded if he had used the tactics of either of the others.

The first wanted to talk with the biggest executive in a large organization. He had fought his way through the ranks until he had got as far as the man's secretary. "Mr. So-and-So does not see people who want jobs," said that young lady.

"I don't want a job," he prevaricated mildly, "I want to talk to him."

The girl let him in.

"Mr. So-and-So," he said, "I don't want a job. I want advice."

His manner was so ingenuous and charming, his earnestness so glowing, that the man at the desk listened while he talked, and then talked a while himself, and ended by giving the young man the position (as well as the advice) that he wanted. But if he had been less attractive personally and the older man had been shrewd enough to see through the ruse (or perhaps he did see through it but made the proper discount for it) or had been opposed to trick methods, the scheme might not have worked so well.

The most universal weakness of intellect lies in the part of the brain which listens to flattery. Very few people like compliments laid on with a trowel, but no man can resist the honest admiration of another if it seems sincere. And since it is the sort of thing that one likes almost above all else he often takes the false coin for the true.

The second young man met the rebuff so familiar to young men looking for their first job, "We want men with experience."

"That's what everybody says," the boy answered, "but what I want to know is how we are going to get that experience if you don't give us a chance."

The older man sympathized, but had no place for the other and told him so.

"What would you do if you were I?" the young man asked as he turned to leave. The other grinned. "Why, I'd work for a firm for a week for nothing," he said, "and show them that they could not get along without me."

The boy stopped. "All right," he said, "let me work for you a week."

The older man had not expected this but he gave the youngster a chance and he made good.

The third young man had reached the point of desperation. He had been out of a job several weeks. He had been trying to get one all that time and had not succeeded. He walked into the employment bureau of a certain concern and said, "I want a job. I want a good job. Not some dinky little place filing letters or picking up chips. If you've got an executive position where there is plenty of work and plenty of responsibility, I want it." They asked him a few questions about what he had been doing and a few more about what he thought he could do, and ended by giving him a desk and an office.

It would be foolish to advise any one to follow any of these plans. Each man must work out his own method, all the better if it is an original one. Most business men like a simple approach without any flourishes. "It is astonishing," says one man whose income runs to six figures, "how many things one can get just by asking for them." The best reporter in America says that he has always found the direct method of approach better than any other. None is infallible but this has the highest percentage of success.

So far as personal appearance is concerned—and this is one of the most important elements in the fashioning of personality—the greatest variations are not due to intrinsic differences in character, nor to differences of feature or form, but to the use and disuse of the bathtub. More sharp than the distinction between labor and capital or between socialism and despotism is that between the people who bathe daily and those who go to the tub only on Saturday night or less often. The people with whom personal cleanliness is a habit find dirt, grime, and sweat revolting. To them "the great unwashed" are repulsive.

"When you teach a man to bathe," says John Leitch in his book on "Industrial Democracy," "you do more than merely teach him to cleanse his body. You introduce him to a new kind of life and create in him a desire for better living."

The month before he began his wonderful work at Tuskegee, Booker Washington spent visiting the Negro families in the part of Alabama where he was to teach. "One of the saddest things I saw during the month of travel which I have described," he writes in his autobiography, "was a young man, who had attended some high school, sitting down in a one-room cabin, with grease on his clothing, filth all around him, and weeds in the yard and garden, engaged in studying a French grammar."

Farther on he writes, "It has been interesting to note the effect that the use of the tooth-brush has had in bringing about a higher degree of civilization among the students. With few exceptions, I have noticed that, if we can get a student to the point where, when the first or second tooth-brush disappears, he of his own motion buys another, I have not been disappointed in the future of that individual. Absolute cleanliness of the body has been insisted upon from the first."

Cleanliness is an attribute of civilization. We find it amusing to read that three or four hundred years ago bathing for pleasure was unknown, that when soap was first invented it was used only for washing clothes, and that even so late as the Seventeenth Century an author compiling a book of rules for the gentleman of that day advises him to wash his hands every day and his face almost as often! In the monasteries bathing was permitted only to invalids and the very old. Perfume was used copiously, and filth and squalor abounded. This even in royal circles. Among the common people conditions were unspeakable.

To-day a gentleman bathes and shaves every day. He keeps his hair brushed, his finger nails immaculate (or as clean as the kind of work which he does permits), his linen is always clean and his shoes are polished. He is not over-fastidious about his clothes, but he has respect enough for himself as well as for the people among whom he lives to want to present as agreeable an appearance as possible. "Dress," wrote Lord Chesterfield to his son, "is a very foolish thing, and yet it is a very foolish thing for a man not to be well-dressed, according to his rank and way of life. . . . The difference in this case between a man of sense and a fop is that the fop values himself upon his dress; and the man of sense laughs at it, and at the same time knows he must not neglect it."

It is a cheap device for a man to trick himself out with lodge pins and fraternity symbols, rings, and badges in the hope that they will open doors for him. Highly ornamental jewelry of any kind is inappropriate. Not many men can off-set a heavy gold watch chain stretched full length across their bosoms, not many can live down a turquoise ring set with pearls, and very few can bear the handicap of a bright gold front tooth. Artists, alone, may gratify their taste for velvet jackets, Tam-o'-Shanters, and Windsor ties, but the privilege is denied business men. Eccentricity of dress usually indicates eccentricity of temper, and we do not want temperamental business men. It is hard enough to get along with authors and artists and musicians. The business man who is wise wears conventional clothes of substantial material in conservative colors. Good sense and good taste demand it.

The time has passed when uncouthness of dress and manner can be taken as a pledge of honesty and good faith. The President of the United States to-day is a well-dressed, well-groomed man, and no one thinks any the less of him for it. Men no longer regard creased trousers, nicely tied cravats, well-chosen collars, and harmonious color combinations as signs of sissiness, snobbishness, or weak-mindedness.

Formal dinners and other ceremonious functions require evening dress. It is the custom, as the Orientals say; and for the sake of other people present if not for his own, a man should undergo the discomfort, if he finds it a discomfort, and many men do, of conforming to it. Holiday attire gives a happy note of festivity which might otherwise be lacking. It is quite possible to point to a number of men who have succeeded in business who were wholly indifferent to matters of dress. But it does not prove anything. Men rise by their strength, not by their weakness. Some men wait until after they have become rich or famous to become negligent of their personal appearance. But it is well to remember that "if Socrates and Aristippus have done aught against custom or good manner, let not a man think he can do the same: for they obtained this license by their great and excellent good parts."

A well-dressed man is so comfortably dressed that he is not conscious of his clothes and so inconspicuously dressed that no one else is conscious of them.

In a good many instances it is not his own dress which bothers a business man so much as it is that of some one else—his stenographer, for instance. Men do not have quite so much opportunity to make themselves ridiculous as women. Their conventions of dress are stricter, and, as a rule, they can express their love of color and ornamentation only in their choice of ties and socks. Girls have practically no restrictions except what happens to be the style at the moment, and a young girl untrained in selecting and combining colors and lines, and making money for the first time in her life, is more likely than not to make herself look more like a Christmas tree than a lily of the field.

The big department stores which employ hundreds of girls to meet and serve their customers have settled the problem for themselves by requiring the girls to wear uniforms. The uniform is very simple; often a certain color during working hours is prescribed, but the girls are permitted to choose their own styles. Other places have women who look after the welfare of the girls and prevent them from laying themselves open to misunderstanding by the way they dress. Large organizations can afford to have a special person to take care of such matters, but in a small office the problem is different.

Of course, a man can always dismiss a girl who dresses foolishly or carelessly, but this is sneaking away from a problem instead of facing it. High-class offices have comparatively little trouble this way. In the first place, they do not attract the frivolous, light-headed, or "tough" girls; in the second place, if such girls come, the atmosphere in which they work either makes them conform to the standards of the office or leave and go somewhere else. If a girl in his office dresses in a way that he considers inappropriate, a man may tactfully suggest that something simpler would be more dignified and more in keeping with business ideals and traditions. But, oh, he must be careful! On no subjcet is one so sensitive as on his personal appearance, and women, perhaps, more so than men.

There is a limit to how far an employer should go in dictating the manner of his employees' dress. When the head of a big Western department store declared that he would discharge all the girls who bobbed their hair, most of us felt that he had gone a bit too far, even while we saw the logic of his position. While it is the only sensible way in the world for a woman to wear her hair the majority of people have not yet come to think so. To the average person, especially to Mrs. Grundy, who is really the most valuable customer a department store has, the impression given by bobbed hair is one of frivolity or eccentricity. The impression given the customer as she enters a store is a most important item; the head of the store knew it, and therefore he placed the ban on bobbed hair. Whichever side we take in this particular case this is true: The business woman should give, like the business man, an impression of dependability, and she cannot do it if her appearance is abnormal, or if her mind is divided between how she is looking and what she is doing.

It is almost funny that we let the faults and mannerisms of other people affect us to such an extent. They are nothing to us, and yet a man can work himself into a perfect frenzy of temper merely by looking at or talking to another who has a fidgety way of moving about, a dainty manner of using his hands, or a general demean-

or that is delicate and ladylike.   Men like what
the magazines call "a red-blooded, two-fisted, he-
man."   But the world is big enough to accom-
modate us all whether the blood in our veins is
red or blue, and it is perfectly silly for a man to
throw himself into a rage over some harmless
creature who happens to exasperate him simply
because he is alive.

It is an altogether different matter when it is
a question of one man taking liberties with another.   Most people object to the physical near-
ness of others.   It is the thing that makes the
New York subways during the rush hours such
a horror.   It is not pleasant to have a person so
near that his breath is against your face, and
there are not many men who enjoy being slapped
on the back, punched in the ribs, or held fast by
a buttonhole or a coat lapel.   A safe rule is
never to touch another person.   He may resent
it.

The garrulous or impertinent talker is almost
as objectionable as the hail-fellow-well-met, slap-
on-the-back fellow.   Charles Dickens has a record of this kind of American in the book which
he wrote after his visit in this country: "Every
button in his clothes said, 'Eh, what's that?   Did
you speak?   Say that again, will you?'   He was
always wide awake, always restless;   always

thirsting for answers; perpetually seeking and never finding. . . .

"I wore a fur great-coat at that time, and before we were well clear of the wharf, he questioned me concerning it, and its price, and where I bought it, and when, and what fur it was, and what it weighed, and what it cost. Then he took notice of my watch, and asked me what *that* cost, and whether it was a French watch, and where I got it, and how I got it, and whether I bought it or had it given me, and how it went and where the keyhole was, and when I wound it, every night or every morning, and whether I ever forgot to wind it at all, and if I did, what then? Where I had been to last, and where I was going next, and where I was going after that, and had I seen the President, and what did he say, and what did I say, and what did he say when I had said that? Eh? Lor' now! Do tell!"

This sort of curiosity is harmless enough, but exasperating, and so childish that one hates to rebuke the person who is asking the foolish questions. There is another kind which is perhaps worse—the man who asks intrusive questions about how much salary another is getting, how old he is (men are as sensitive on this subject as women) and so on and on. It is perfectly legitimate to refuse to answer any question to which one does not wish to reply.   Every man has a right to mental privacy even when he is denied, as he is in so many modern offices, any other kind of privacy.

A loud or boisterous person is objectionable. Many times this is through carelessness, but sometimes, as when a man recounts the story of his dinner with Mr. Brown, who is a national figure, in a voice so loud that all the people in the car or room or whatever place he happens to be in, can hear him, it is deliberate.   The careless person is the one who discusses personalities aloud in elevators, on the train, and in all manner of public places.   Exchanging gossip is a pretty low form of indoor sport and exchanging it aloud so that everybody can hear makes it worse than ever.   Names should never be mentioned in a conversation in a place where strangers can overhear, especially if the connection is an unpleasant one.   Private opinions should never be aired in public places (except from a platform).

The highly argumentative or aggressive person is another common type of nuisance.   He usually raises his voice, thus drowning out the possibility of interruption, and talks with so much noise and so many vigorous gestures that he seems to try to make up for his lack of intellect by an excess of tumult. Arguments have never yet convinced anybody of the truth, and it is a very unpleasant method to try. Most arguments are about religion or politics and even if they were settled nothing would be accomplished. In the Middle Ages men used to debate about the number of angels that could stand on the point of a pin. Hours and hours were wasted and learned scholars were brought into the discussion, which was carried forward as seriously as if it were a debate between the merits of the Republican and Democratic parties. Suppose they had settled it. Would it have mattered?

One of the most offensive public plagues is the man who leaves a trail of untidiness behind him. No book of etiquette, not even a book of business etiquette, could counsel eating on the streets in spite of the historic and inspiring example of Mr. Benjamin Franklin walking down the streets of Philadelphia with a loaf of bread under each arm while he munched from a third which he held in his hand. One can forgive a man, however, if he, feeling the need of nourishment, eats a bar of chocolate if he takes great care to put the wrappings somewhere out of the way. No man with any civic pride will scatter peanut hulls, cigarette boxes, chocolate wrappings, raisin boxes, and other débris along the streets, in the cars, on the stairs, and even on the floors of office build-ings. Garbage cans and waste-baskets were made to take care of these things.

Tidiness is worth more to a business man than most of them realize. In the first place it gives a favorable impression to a person coming in from the outside, and, in the second place, it helps those on the inside to keep things straight. Folders for correspondence, card indexes, memo-randum files and other similar devices are essen-tial to the orderly transaction of business.

Keeping ashes and scraps of paper off the floor may seem trifles, but such trifles go far to-ward making the atmosphere, which is another word for personality, of an office. Some men have secretaries who take care of their desks and papers and supervise the janitor who cleans the floors and windows, but those who do not, find that they can manage better when they have a place to put things and put them there.

Nothing has more to do with making a gentle-man than a courteous and considerate attitude toward women. In business a man should show practically the same deference toward a woman that he does in society. Any man can be polite to a woman he is anxious to please, the girl he loves, for instance, but it takes a gentleman to be polite to every woman, especially to those who work for him, those over whom he exercises authority.

It is unnecessary for a man to rise every time one of the girls in his office enters his private audience room, but he should always rise to receive a visitor, whether it is a man or woman, and should ask the visitor to be seated before he sits down himself. In witheringly hot weather a man may go without his coat even if his entire office force consists of girls, but he should never receive a guest in his shirt sleeves. He should listen deferentially to what the visitor has to say, but if she becomes too voluble or threatens to stay too long or if there is other business waiting for him, he may (if he can) cut short her conversation. When she is ready to go he should rise and conduct her to the door or to the elevator, as the case may be, and ring the bell for her. He cannot, of course, do this if his visitors are frequent, if their calls are about matters of trifling importance, or if he is working under high pressure.

We once had an English visitor here in America who thought our manners were outrageously bad, but there was one point on which we won a perfect score. "Any lady," he said, "may travel alone, from one end of the United States to the other, and be certain of the most courteous and considerate treatment everywhere. Nor did I ever once, on any occasion, anywhere, during my rambles in America, see a woman exposed to the slightest act of rudeness, incivility, or even inat-, tention." Conditions have changed since then. Women had not left their homes to go into offices and factories, but unless we can hold to the standard described by the Englishman, the change has not been for the better, for any of the people concerned.

Since the Victorian era our ideas of what constitutes an act of rudeness have been modified. Then it would have been unthinkable that a woman should remain standing in a coach while men were seated. Now it is possible for a man to keep his place while a woman swings from a strap and defend himself on the grounds that he has worked harder during the day than she (how he knows is more than we can say), and that he has just as much right (which is certainly true) as any one else. Yet it is a gracious and a chivalrous act for a man to offer a woman his place on a car, and it is very gratifying to see that hundreds of them, even in the cities, where life goes at its swiftest pace and people live always in a hurry, surrender their seats in favor of the women who, like themselves, are going to work. Old people, afflicted people, men and women who are carrying children in their arms, and other people who obviously need to sit down are nearly always given precedence over the rest of us. This is, of course, as it should be.

But the heart of what constitutes courtesy has not changed and never will. It is exactly what it was on that day nearly four hundred years ago when Sir Philip Sidney, mortally wounded on the field of Zutphen, gave his last drop of water to the dying soldier who lay near him and said, "Thy need is greater than mine."

V

TABLE MANNERS

IN THE old books of etiquette in the chapter on table manners the authors used to state that it was not polite to butter your bread with your thumb, to rub your greasy fingers on the bread you were about to eat, or to rise from the table with a toothpick in your mouth like a bird that is about to build her nest. We have never seen any one butter his bread with his thumb, but——

There are in the United States nearly five million people who can neither read nor write. We have no statistics but we venture to say there are as many who eat with their knives. There are people among us—and they are not all immigrants in the slum districts or Negroes in the poorer sections of the South—who do not know what a napkin is, who think the proper way to eat an egg is to hold it in the hand like a piece of candy, and bite it, the egg having previously been fried on both sides until it is as stiff and as hard as a piece of bristol board, who would not recognize a salad if they saw one, and who have never heard of after-dinner coffee.

Very few of them are people of wealth, but an astonishing number of successful business men were born into such conditions. They had no training in how to handle a knife and fork and they probably never read a book of etiquette, but they had one faculty, which is highly developed in nearly every person who lifts himself above the crowd, and that is observation.

In addition to this a young man is very fortunate, especially if his way of life is cast among people whose manners are different from those to which he has been accustomed, if he has a friend whom he can consult, not only about table manners but about matters of graver import as well. And he should not be embarrassed to ask questions. The disgrace, if disgrace it could be called, lies only in ignorance.

A number of years ago a young man who was the prospective heir to a fortune—this charming story is in Charles Dickens's wonderful novel, "Great Expectations"—went up to London for the express purpose of learning to be a gentleman. It fell about that almost as soon as he arrived he was thrown into the company of a delightful youth who had already attained the minor graces of polite society. Very much in earnest about what he had set out to do, and blessed besides with a goodish bit of common sense, he explained his situation to Herbert, for that was the other boy's name, mentioned the fact that he had been brought up by a blacksmith in a country place, that he knew practically nothing of the ways of politeness, and that he would take it as a great kindness if Herbert would give him a hint whenever he saw him at a loss or going wrong.

" 'With pleasure,' said he, 'though I venture to prophesy that you'll want very few hints.' "

They went in to dinner together, a regular feast of a dinner it seemed to the ex-blacksmith's apprentice, and after a while began to talk about the benefactress who, they believed, had made it possible.

" 'Let me introduce the topic,' began Herbert, who had been watching Pip's table manners for some little time, 'by mentioning that in London it is not the custom to put the knife in the mouth—for fear of accidents—and that while the fork is reserved for that use it is not put further in than necessary. It is scarcely worth mentioning, only it's as well to do as other people do. Also, the spoon is not generally used over-hand but under. This has two advantages. You get at your mouth better (which after all is the objcet), and you save a good deal of the attitude of opening oysters on the part of the right elbow.'

"He offered these suggestions (said Pip) in such a lively way, that we both laughed and I scarcely blushed."

The conversation and the dinner continued and the friendship grew apace. Presently Herbert broke off to observe that "society as a body does not expect one to be so strictly conscientious in emptying one's glass, as to turn it bottom upwards with the rim on one's nose."

"I had been doing this," Pip confessed, "in an excess of attention to his recital. I thanked him, and apologized. He said, 'Not at all,' and resumed."

This was written many years ago but neither in life nor in literature is there a more beautiful example of perfect courtesy than that given by Herbert Pocket when he took the blacksmith's boy in hand and began his education in the art of being a gentleman. Not only was he at perfect ease himself but—and this is the important point —he put the blacksmith's boy at ease.

It is worth remarking, by way of parenthesis, that Herbert's father was a gentleman. "It is a principle of his," declared the boy, "that no man who was not a true gentleman at heart, ever was, since the world began, a true gentleman in manner.   He says, no varnish can hide the grain of the wood; and that the more varnish you put on, the more the grain will express itself."

The American table service is not complicated.   Any intelligent person who knows the points covered by Herbert Pocket, who knows that one should not cut up all of his meat at the same time but mouthful by mouthful as he needs it, that it is not customary to butter a whole slice of bread at once nor to plaster cheese over the entire upper surface of a cracker, can by a dint of watching how other people do it find his way without embarrassment through even the most elaborate array of table implements.   The easiest way to acquire good table manners (or good manners of any other kind, as far as that goes) is to form the habit of observing how the people who manage these things most gracefully go about it.   It is best to begin early.   To use one of David Harum's expressive maxims, "Ev'ry hoss c'n do a thing better 'n' spryer if he's ben broke to it as a colt."

Eating should be, and, as a matter of fact, is, when one follows his usual custom, an unconscious process like the mechanical part of reading or writing.   It is only when he is trying to be a bit more formal or fastidious than is habitual with him that a man gets tangled, so to speak, in the tines of his fork.

Cooking is one of the fine arts. Poets, painters, sculptors, musicians, and millionaires have always paid tribute to it as such—and so is dining. Like a great many other arts it was first developed among royal circles, and there was a time when the king resented the idea of a commoner being able to dine with grace and elegance. Since then it has become democratized, and now there are no restrictions except those which a man places about himself. And there is no earthly (or heavenly) reason why a man should not eat in the way which society has established as correct, and a good many reasons why he should.

Physicians—and this is the strongest argument we know—might advance their plea on the grounds of good health. In this case we find, as we do in a number of others, that what good manners declares should be done is heartily endorsed at the same time by good sense. It is only among people of blunted sensibilities that nice table manners count for nothing; for

> There's no reproach among swine, d'you see,
> For being a bit of a swine.

Among business men it is often perplexing to know whom and when to invite. Generally speaking, the older man or the man with the superior position takes the initiative, but there are an infinite number of exceptions. Generally speaking, also, the man who is resident in a place entertains the one who is visiting, but there are infinite exceptions to this as well, especially in the case of traveling salesman. All courtesy is mutual, and it is almost obligatory upon the salesman who has been entertained to return the courtesy in kind. Such invitations should be tendered after a transaction is completed rather than before. The burden of table courtesy falls upon the man who is selling rather than the one who is buying, probably because he is the one to whom the obvious profit accrues.

Social affairs among the wives of business men which grow out of the business relations of their husbands follow the same rules as almost any other social affairs. Nearly always it is the wife of the man with the higher position who issues the first invitation, and it is permissible for her to invite a woman whom she does not know personally if she is the wife of a business friend of her husband.

The biggest hindrance to the establishment of good manners among business men is the everlasting hurry in which they (and all the rest of us) live. There must first of all be leisure, not perhaps to the extent advocated by a delightful literary gentleman of having three hours for lunch every day, but time enough to sit down and relax. Thousands of business men dash out to lunch—bad manners are at their worst in the middle of the day—as if they were stopping off at a railroad junction with twenty minutes to catch a train and had used ten of them checking baggage. And they do not always do it because they are in a hurry. They have so thoroughly developed the habit of living in a frenzied rush that even when they have time to spare they cannot slow down.

Pleasant surroundings are desirable. It is much easier to dine in a quiet spacious room where the linen is white and the china is thin, the silver is genuine silver, and the service is irreproachable, than in a crowded restaurant where thick dishes rattle down on white-tiled tables from the steaming arms of the flurried waitress, where there is no linen, but only flimsy paper napkins (which either go fluttering to the floor or else form themselves into damp wads on the table), where the patrons eat ravenously and untidily, and where the atmosphere is dense with the fumes of soup and cigarettes. But luxury in eating is expensive and most of us must, perforce, go to the white-tiled places. And the art of dining is not a question of what one has to eat—it may be beans or truffles—or where one eats it—from a tin bucket or a mahogany table—it all depends upon *how;* and the man who can eat in a "hash-house," an "arm-chair joint," a "bean-erie," a cafeteria, a three-minute doughnut stand or any of the other quick-lunch places in as mannerly a way as if he were dining in a hotel *de luxe* has, we think, a pretty fair claim to the title of gentleman.

The responsibility for a dinner lies with the host. If his guest has had the same social training that he has or is accustomed to better things he will have comparatively little trouble. All he can do is to give him the best within his means *without apology.* We like to present ourselves in the best possible light (it is only human) and for this reason often carry our friends to places we cannot afford. This imposes upon them the necessity of returning the dinner in kind, and the vicious circle swings around, each person in it grinding his teeth with rage but not able to find his way out. Entertaining is all right so long as it is a useful adjunct to business, but when it becomes a burden in itself it is time to call a halt.

Smoking during and immediately after a meal is very pleasing to the man who likes tobacco, but if he has a guest (man or woman) who objects to the smell of it he must wait until later. On the other hand if his guest likes to smoke and he does not he should insist upon his doing so. It is a trifling thing but politeness consists largely of yielding gracefully in trifles.

Old-fashioned gentlemen held it discourteous to mention money at table, but in this degenerate age no subject is taboo except those that would be taboo in any decent society. Obviously when men meet to talk over business they cannot leave money out of the discussion. In a number of firms the executives have lunch together, meeting in a group for perhaps the only time during the day. It helps immeasurably to coördinate effort, but it sometimes fails to make the lunch hour the restful break in the middle of the day which it should be. It is generally much more fun and of much more benefit to swap fish stories and hunting yarns than to go over the details of the work in the publicity department or to formulate the plans for handling the Smith and Smith proposition. Momentous questions should be thrust aside until later, and the talk should be—well, *talk,* not arguing, quarreling, or scandal-mongering. The subject does not greatly matter except that it should be something in which all of the people at the table are interested.   Whistler was once asked what he would do if he were out at dinner and the conversation turned to the Mexican War, and some one asked him the date of a certain battle.   "Do?" he replied.   "Why, I would refuse to associate with people who could talk of such things at dinner!"

Polite society has always placed a high value on table manners, but it is only recently that they have come to play so large a part in business. Some one has said that you cannot mix business and friendship.   It would be nearer the truth to say that you cannot separate them.   More and more it is becoming the habit to transact affairs over the table, and a very pleasant thing it is, too.   Aside from the coziness and warmth which comes from breaking bread together one is free from the interruptions and noise of the office, and many a commercial acquaintance has ripened into a friend and many a business connection has been cemented into something stronger through the genial influence of something good to eat and drink.   It is, of course, a mistake to depend too much upon one's social gifts.   They are very pleasant and helpful but the work of the world is done in offices, not on golf links or in dining rooms.   We have little patience with the man who sets his nose to the grindstone and does not take it away until death comes in between, but we have just as little with the man who has never touched the grindstone.

Stories go the rounds of executives who choose their subordinates by asking them out to lunch and watching the way they eat. One man always calls for celery and judges his applicant by what he does with it. If he eats only the tender parts the executive decides that he is extravagant, at least with other people's money, but if he eats the whole stalk, green leaves and all, he feels sure that he has before him a man of economy, common sense, and good judgment! The story does not say what happens when the young man refuses celery altogether. Another uses cherry pie as his standard and judges the young man by what he does with the pits. There are three ways to dispose of them. They may be lowered from the mouth with the spoon, they may be allowed to drop unaided, or they may be swallowed. The last course is not recommended. The first is the only one that will land a job. But tests like this work both ways and one is rather inclined to congratulate the young men who were turned down than those who were accepted.

All this aside, an employer does want to know something about the table manners of an employee who is to meet and dine with his customers. An excellent salesman may be able to convince a man of good breeding and wide social training if he tucks his napkin into his bosom, drinks his soup with a noise, and eats his meat with his knife, but the chances are against it.

A man who is interested heart and soul in one thing will think in terms of it, will have it constantly in his mind and on the tip of his tongue. But the man of one subject, whatever that subject may be, is a bore. It is right that a man should live in his work, but he must also live outside of it. One of the most tragic chapters in the history of American life is the one which tells of the millions and millions of men who became so immersed in business affairs that they lost sight of everything else. The four walls of the narrow house which in the end closes around us all could not more completely have cut them off from the light of day. It is a long procession and it has not ended—that line of men passing single file like convicts down the long gray vaults of business, business, business, with never a thought for the stars or the moon or books or trees or flowers or music or life or love—nothing but what casts a shadow over that dismal corridor.

These are dead men with no thought
Of things that are not sold or bought.

*   *   *

In their bodies there is breath,
But their souls are steeped in death.

It is not a cheerful picture to contemplate (and it seems a good long way away from table manners), but the men who form it are more to be pitied than blamed.   They are blind.

VI

TELEPHONES AND FRONT DOORS

"IF THE outside of a place is not all right," says a man who spends the greater part of his time visiting business houses and talking with business men, "the chances are that it is not worth while to go inside."

There are three ways of getting inside: by letter (which has a chapter to itself), by the front door, and by telephone. And there are more complaints against the telephone way than either or both the others, which is perfectly natural, since it is the most difficult to manage. In the first place, it requires good behavior from three people at the same time, and that is a good deal to expect. Secondly, they cannot see one another—they are like blind people talking together—and no one of them can do his part unless the other two do theirs. In the third place, the instrument is a lifeless thing, and when something goes wrong with it it rouses the helpless fury inspired by all inanimate objects which interfere with our comfort—like intermittent alarm clocks, collar buttons that roll under the furniture, and flivvers that go dead without reason in the middle of country roads. In each case whatever one does has no effect. The alarm clock continues to ring (unless one gets out of bed to shut it off, which is worse than letting it ring), the collar button remains hid in the darkest part of the room, the flivver remains stuck in the muddiest part of the road, and the telephone is worst of all, for the source of the trouble is usually several miles away and there is no means of getting at it.

The telephone is a nuisance—no one denies it—but it is a necessity also—no one denies that, either—and one of the greatest conveniences in an age of great conveniences. Some of the disagreeable features connected with it cannot be done away with but must be accepted with as much tranquility as we can master, like the terrific noise which an aëroplane makes or the trail of smoke and cinders which a railway train leaves behind. The one who is calling, for instance, cannot know that he is the tenth or eleventh person who has called the man at the other end of the wire in rapid succession, that his desk is piled high with correspondence which must be looked over, signed, and sent out before noon, that the advertising department is waiting for him to O. K. their plans for a campaign which should have been launched the week before, that an important visitor is sitting in the library growing more impatient every minute, and that his temper has been filed down to the quick by an assortment of petty worries. (Of course, no office should be run like this, but it sometimes happens in the best of them.)

Some one has said that we are all like islands shouting at each other across a sea of misunderstanding, and this was long before telephones were thought of. It is hard enough to make other people understand what we mean, even with the help of facial expression and gestures, and over the wire the difficulty is increased a hundred fold. For telephoning rests upon a delicate adjustment between human beings by means of a mechanical apparatus, and it takes clear thinking, patience, and courtesy to bring it about.

The telephone company began its career some few years ago unhampered by the traditions to which the earlier corporations were slave, the old "public be damned" idea. Their arbitrary methods had brought them to grief, and the new concern, with a commendable regard for the lessons taught by the experience of others, inaugurated a policy of usefulness, service, and courtesy. The inside history of the telephone is one of constant watchfulness, careful management, and continuous improvement; and every improvement has meant better service to the public. (We are not trying to advertise the telephone company. We realize that it has been guilty, like every other business, of manifold sins.)

Even the fact that there is a telephone girl instead of a telephone boy is due to the alertness and good business sense of the company. To put a boy before a switchboard and expect him not to pull it apart to see how it was made; or to place him in a position to entertain himself by connecting the wrong parties and listening to the impolite names they called each other and expect him not to do it, would be expecting the laws of nature to reverse themselves. The telephone company tried it—for a while. They discovered, besides, that a boy will not "take" what a girl will. It makes no difference what goes wrong with a connection, the subscriber blames the operator when many times the operator, especially the one he is talking to, has had nothing to do with it. The girls have learned to hold their tempers (not always, but most of the time), but when boys had charge of the switchboards and the man at the end of the wire yelled, "You cut me off!" and the youngster had not, he denied it hotly: "You're a liar! I didn't!" The subscriber would not stand for this, angry words flew back and forth, and more than once the indignant young operator located the subscriber (not a very difficult thing for him to do) and went around to settle things in person. Words were not always the only weapons used.

If this had continued the telephone would never have become a public utility. People would have looked upon it as an ingenious device but not of universal practical value. As it is, good salesmanship and efficient service first elevated a plaything to a luxury and then reduced the luxury to a necessity. And it was possible not only because the mechanism itself is a miraculous thing but because it has had back of it an intelligent human organization working together as a unit.

We say this deliberately, knowing that the reader will think of the times when the trouble he has had in getting the number he wanted has made him think there was not a thimbleful of intelligence among all of the people associated with the entire telephone company. But considering the body of employees as a whole the standard of courteous and competent service is extraordinarily high. The public is impatient and prone to remember bad connections instead of good ones. It is ignorant also and has very small conception of what a girl at central is doing. And it is quick to blame her for faults of its own.

One of the worst features of telephone service is the fact that when one is angry or exasperated he seldom quarrels with the right person. Some time ago a man was waked in the middle of the night by the ringing of the telephone bell. He got out of bed to answer it and discovered that the man was trying to get another number. He went back to bed and to sleep. The telephone bell rang again, and again he got out of bed to answer it. It was the same man trying to get the same number. He went to bed and back to sleep. The telephone bell rang the third time, he got out of bed again and answered it again and found that it was still the same man trying to get the same number! "I wasn't very polite the third time," he confessed when he told about it. But the poor fellow at the other end of the wire probably had just as touching a story to tell, for unless it had been very important for him to get the number he would hardly have been so persistent. The girl at the switchboard may have had a story of her own, but what it

was is one of those things which, as Lord Dun-
dreary used to say, nobody can find out.

The girls who enter the service of the New
York Telephone Company (and the same thing
is true in the other branches of the telephone service, especially in big cities where there are large
groups to work with) are carefully selected by
an employment bureau and sent to a school
where they are thoroughly grounded in the mechanical part of their work and the ideals for
which the company stands. They are not placed
on a regular switchboard until they have proved
themselves efficient on the dummy switchboard,
and then it is with instructions to be courteous
though the heavens fall (though they do not express it exactly that way). "It is the best place
in the world to learn self-control," one of the
operators declares, and any one who has ever
watched them at work will add, "Concentration,
also." One of the most remarkable sights in
New York is a central exchange where a hundred or more girls are working at lightning
speed, undisturbed by the low murmur around
them, intent only on the switchboard in front of
them, making something like five hundred connections a minute.

They are a wonderfully level-headed group,
these telephone girls, wonderfully unlike their

clinging-vine Victorian grandmothers. They do not know how to cling. If a man telephones that he has been shot, the girl who receives the call does not faint. She sends him a doctor instead and takes the next call almost without the loss of a second. If a woman wants a policeman to get some burglars out of the house, she sends her one; if some one telephones that a house is burning, she calls out the fire department—and goes straight on with her work. Now and then something spectacular happens to bring the splendid courage of the girls at the switchboards to the attention of the public, such as the magnificent service they gave from the exchange located a few feet from Wall Street on the day of the explosion, but ordinarily it passes, like most of the other good things in life, without comment.

The New York Telephone Company tries to keep its girls healthy and happy. At regular intervals they are given rest periods. Attractive rooms are prepared for them, tastefully furnished, well-lighted, and filled with comfortable chairs, good books, and magazines. Substantial meals are supplied in the middle of the day at a nominal charge. Special entertainments are planned from time to time, and best of all, the play time is kept absolutely distinct from the work time, a condition which makes for happiness as well as usefulness.

The girls are not perfect, they are not infallible. And they are only a third part of a telephone call. They work under difficulties at a task which is not an easy one, and their efficiency does not rest with them alone but with the people whom they serve as well.

A telephone call begins with the subscriber. Very few people understand the intricate system of cable and dynamos, vacuum tubes, coil racks, storage batteries, transmitters and generators which enable them to talk from a distance, and a good many could not understand them even if they were explained. Fortunately it is not necessary that they should. The subscriber's part is very simple.

He should first make sure that he is calling the right number. In New York City alone, forty-eight thousand wrong numbers are asked for every day by subscribers who have not consulted the telephone directory first, or who have unconsciously transposed the digits in a number. For example, a number such as 6454 can easily be changed to 6544. The telephone directory is a safe guide, much more so than an old letter or bill head or an uncertain memory. Information may be called if the number is not in the directory, but

one should be definite even with her.   She cannot supply the number of Mr. What-you-may-
call-it or of Mr. Thing-um-a-bob or of Mr. Smith
who lives down near the railroad station, and she
cannot give the telephone number of a house
which has no telephone in it.   She has no right
to answer irrelevant questions; is, in fact, prohibited from doing so.   Her business is to furnish numbers and she cannot do it efficiently if
she is expected also to explain why a cat has
whiskers, how to preserve string beans by drying
them, what time it is, what time the train leaves
for Wakefield, or what kind of connection can be
made at Jones's Junction.

In calling a number the name of the exchange
should be given first.   The number itself should
be called with a slight pause between the hundreds and the tens, thus, "Watkins—pause—
five, nine—pause—hundred" for "Watkins
5900" or "Murray Hill—pause—four, two—
pause—six, three" for "Murray Hill 4263."
The reason for this is that the switchboard before which the operator sits is honeycombed
with tiny holes arranged in sections of one hundred each.   Each section is numbered and
each of the holes within it is the termination
of a subscriber's line.   In locating "Watkins
5900" the girl first finds the section labelled "59"

and then the "00" hole in that section, and if the "59" is given first she has found it by the time the subscriber has finished calling the number.

The number should be pronounced slowly and distinctly.

When the operator repeats it the subscriber should acknowledge it, and if she repeats it incorrectly, should stop her and give her the number again. And he should always remember, however difficult it may be to make her understand, that he is talking to a girl, a human being, and that the chances are ten to one that the poor connection is not her fault.

To recall the operator in case the wrong person is connected it is only necessary to move the receiver hook slowly up and down. She may not be able to attend to the recall at once but jiggling the hook angrily up and down will not get her any sooner. In fact, the more furious the subscriber becomes the less the girl knows about it, for the tiny signal light fails to register except when the hook is moved slowly; or if the switchboard is one where the operator is signalled by a little disk which falls over a blank space the disk fails to move down but remains quivering almost imperceptibly in its usual position.

After he has placed a call a man should wait at the telephone or near it until the connection is made. Too many men have a way of giving their secretaries a number to send through and then wandering off somewhere out of sight so that when the person is finally connected he has to wait several minutes while the secretary locates the man who started the call. It is the acme of discourtesy to keep any one waiting in this manner. It implies that your time is much more valuable than his, which may be true, but it is hardly gracious to shout it in so brazen a fashion.

It has been estimated that in New York City alone, more than a full business year is lost over the telephone every day between sunrise and sunset. There are 3,800,000 completed connections made every day. Out of each hundred, six show a delay of a minute or more before the person called answers. In each day this amounts to a delay of 228,000 connections. Two hundred and twenty-eight thousand minutes (and sometimes the delay amounts to much more than a minute) is the equivalent of 475 days of eight hours each, or as the gentleman who compiled these interesting statistics has it, a business year and a third with all the Sundays and holidays intact. In the course of a year it amounts to more than all the business days that have elapsed since Columbus discovered America!

It may be argued that we would be better off if we lost more than a year every day and did all our work at more leisurely pace. This may be, but the time to rest is not when the telephone bell is ringing.

The telephone on a business man's desk should always be facing him and it should not be tricked out with any of the patent devices except those sanctioned by the company. Most of them lessen instead of increase efficiency. A woman in her home where calls are infrequent may hide her telephone behind a lacquered screen or cover it with pink taffeta ruffles, but in a business office it is best to make no attempts to beautify it. It is when it is unadorned that the ugly little instrument gives its best service.

There should always be a pad and pencil at hand so that the message (if there is one) can be taken down without delay. The person at the other end probably has not time (and certainly has not inclination) to wait until you have fumbled through the papers on your desk and the rubbish in the drawers to locate something to write on and something to write with.

"Hello" is a useless and obsolescent form of response in business offices. The name of the firm, of the department, or of the man himself, or of all three, according to circumstances, should be given.   When there is a private operator to take care of the calls she answers with the name of the firm, Blank and Blank.   If the person at the other end of the wire says, "I want the Advertising department," she connects them and the man there answers with "Advertising department." The other then may ask for the manager, in which case the manager answers with his name.   It is easy to grow impatient under all these relays, but a complicated connection involving half a dozen people before the right one is reached can be accomplished in less than a minute if each person sends it straight through without stopping to exchange a number of "Helloes" like a group of Swiss yodelers, or to ask a lot of unnecessary questions.

It is not necessary to scream over the telephone.   The mouth should be held close to the transmitter and the words should be spoken carefully.   In an open office where there are no partitions between the desks one should take especial pains to keep his voice modulated.   One person angrily spluttering over the telephone can paralyze the work of all the people within a radius of fifty feet.   If it were a necessary evil we could make ourselves grow accustomed to it. But it is not. And there is already enough unavoidable wear and tear during the course of a business day without adding this.

"Hello, what do you want?" is no way to answer a call. No decent person would speak even to a beggar at his door in this way and the visitor over the telephone, whoever he is, is entitled to a cordial greeting. *The voice with the smile wins.*

An amusing story is told of a man in Washington who was waked one evening about eleven o'clock by the telephone bell. At first he swore that he would not answer it but his wife insisted that it might be something very important, and finally, outraged and angry, he blundered through the dark across the room and into the hall, jerked down the receiver and yelled, "Hello!" His wife, who was listening tensely for whatever ill news might be forthcoming, was perfectly amazed to hear him saying in the next breath, in the most dulcet tones he had ever used, "Oh, how do you do, I'm *so* glad you called. Oh, delightful. Charmed. I'm sure she will be, too. Thank you. Yes, indeed. So good of you. *Good*-bye." It was the wife of the President of the United States asking him and his wife to dinner at the White House.

If the person calling is given the wrong department he should be courteously transferred to the right one. Courteously, and not with a brusque, "You've got the wrong party" or "I'm not the man you want" but with "Just a minute, please, and I'll give you Mr. Miller."

The time when people are rudest over the telephone is when some one breaks in on the wire. It might be just as well to remember that people do not interrupt intentionally, and the intruder is probably as disconcerted as the man he has interrupted. If he had inadvertently opened the wrong door in a business office the man inside would not have yelled, "Get out of here," but over the telephone he will shriek, "Get off the wire" in a tone he would hardly use to drive the cow out of a cabbage patch.

In an effort to secure better manners among their subscribers the telephone company has asked them to try to visualize the person at the other end of the wire and to imagine that they are talking face to face. Many times a man will say things over the telephone—rude, profane, angry, insulting things, which he would not dream of saying if he were actually before the man he is talking to. And to make it worse he is often so angry that he does not give the other a chance to explain his side of it, at least not until he has said all that he has to say, and even then he not infrequently slams the receiver down on the hook as soon as he has finished!

Listening on a wire passes over from the field of courtesy into that of ethics. On party lines in the country it is not considered a heinous offense to eavesdrop over the telephone, but the conversation there is for the most part harmless neighborhood gossip and it does not matter greatly who hears it. In business it is different. But it is practically impossible for any one except the operator to overhear a conversation except by accident, and it is a misdemeanor punishable by law for her to give a message to any one other than the person for whom it was intended.

In every office there should be a large enough mechanical equipment manned by an efficient staff to take care of the telephone traffic without delay. "The line is busy" given in answer to a call three or four times will send the person who is calling to some other place to have his wants looked after.

Few places appreciate the tremendous volume of business that comes in by way of telephone or the possibilities which it offers to increase business opportunities. They are as short-sighted as the department store which, a good many years ago, when telephones were new, had them in-

stalled but took them out after a few weeks because the clerks were kept so busy taking orders
over them that they did not have time to attend
to the customers who came into the store!

Another important vantage point which, like
the telephone, suffers from neglect is the reception desk.   Millions of dollars' worth of business is lost every year and perfect sandstorms
and cyclones of animosity are generated because
business men have not yet learned the great
value of having the right kind of person to receive visitors.   To the strangers who come—and
among the idlers and swindlers and beggars who
assail every successful business house are poten-
tial good friends and customers—this person
represents the firm,—is, for the time being, the
firm itself.

It is very childish for a man to turn away from
a reception desk because he does not like the manner of the person behind it, but business men, sensible ones at that, do it every day.   Pleasant connections of years' standing are sometimes broken
off and valuable business propositions are carried
to rival concerns because of indifferent or insolent
treatment at the front door.   Only a short time
ago an advertising agency lost a contract for
which it had been working two years on account
of the way the girl at the door received the man

who came to place it. He dropped in without previous appointment and was met by a blonde young lady with highly tinted cheeks who tilted herself forward on the heels of her French pumps and pertly inquired what he wanted. He told her. "Mr. Hunt isn't in." "When will he be back?" "I don't know," and she swung around on the impossible heels. The man deliberated a moment and then swung around on his heels (which were very flat and sensible) and carried the contract to another agency. Instances of this kind might be multiplied. Some business men would have persisted until they got what they wanted from the young lady. Others would have angrily reported her to the head of her office, but the majority would have acted as this man did.

Most men (and women), whether they are in business or not, do not underestimate their own importance and they like to feel that the rest of the world does not either. They do not like to be kept waiting; they like to be received with a nice deference, not haughtily; they do not like to be sent to the wrong department; and they love (and so do we all) talking to important people. Realizing this, banks and trust companies and other big organizations have had to appoint nearly as many vice-presidents as there were second-lieutenants during the war to take care of their self-important visitors. Even those whose time is not worth ten cents (a number of them are women) like to be treated as if it were worth a great deal. It is, for the most part, an innocent desire which does no one any special harm, and any business that sets out to serve the public (and there is no other kind) has to take into account all the caprices of human vanity. We cannot get away from it. Benjamin Franklin placed humility among the virtues he wished to cultivate, but after a time declared it impossible. "For," he said, "if I overcame pride I would be proud of my humility."

Courtesy is the first requirement of the business host or hostess and after that, intelligence. Some business houses make the mistake of putting back of the reception desk a girl who has proved herself too dull-witted to serve anywhere else. The smiling idiot with which this country (and others) so abounds may be harmless and even useful if she is kept busy behind the lines, but, placed out where she is a buffer between the house and the outside world, she is a positive affliction. She may be pleasant enough, but the caller who comes for information and can get nothing but a smile will go away feeling about as cheerful as if he had stuck his hand into a jar of honey when he was a mile or so away from soap, water, and towel.

A litter of office boys sprawling untidily over the desks and chairs in the reception room is as bad, and a snappy young lady of the "Now see here, kid" variety is worse.

The position is not an easy one, especially in places where there is a constant influx of miscellaneous callers, and it is hardly fair to ask a young girl to fill it. In England they use elderly men and in a number of offices over here, too. Their age and manner automatically protect them (and incidentally their firms) from many undesirables that a boy or girl in the same position would have considerable difficulty in handling. And they lend the place an air of dignity and reserve quite impossible with a youngster.

In some offices, especially in those where large amounts of money are stored or handled, there are door men in uniform and often plain clothes huskies near the entrances to protect the people (and the money) on the inside from cranks and crooks and criminals. In others, a physician's office, for instance, or any small office where the people who are likely to come are of the gentler sort, a young girl with a pleasing manner will do just as well as and perhaps better than any one else. In big companies where there are many departments, it is customary to maintain a regular bureau of information to which the caller who is not sure whom or what he wants is first directed, but the majority of businesses have only one person who is delegated to receive the people who come and either direct them to the person they want to see or turn them aside.

Most of them must be turned aside. If the stage managers in New York interviewed all the girls who want to see them, they would have no time left for anything else, and the same thing is true of nearly every man who is prominent in business or in some other way. (Charlie Chaplin received 73,000 letters during the first three days he was in England. Suppose he had personally read each of them!) Hundreds of people must be turned away, but every person who approaches a firm either to get something from it or to give something to it has a right to attention. Men are in business to work, not to entertain, and they must protect themselves. But the people who are turned away must be turned away courteously, and the business house which has found some one who can do it has cause to rise and give thanks.

VII

TRAVELING AND SELLING

THE etiquette of traveling includes very few points not covered by the general laws of good behavior. Keeping one's place in line before the ticket window, having money ready and moving aside as quickly as possible instead of lingering to converse with the ticket-seller about train schedules and divers other interesting subjects are primary rules. It is permissible to make sure that the train is the right one before getting on it, but it is unnecessary to do it more than half a dozen times. When the sign over the gate says "Train for Bellevue" it probably *is* the train for Bellevue, and when the guard at the gate repeats that it is the train for Bellevue the chances are that he is telling the truth.

An experienced traveler usually carries very little baggage. A lot of suitcases and grips are bothersome, not only to the one who has charge of them, but also to those who are cramped into small quarters because of them. A traveler may make himself as comfortable as he likes so

long as it is not at the expense of the other passengers.   If they object to an open window the
window must stay down.   Lounging over a seat
is bad form, especially if there is some one else in
it.   So is prowling from one end of the car to
the other.   Besides, it makes some people nervous.   Snoring is impolite and so is talking in
one's sleep, but they are beyond remedy.   Talking with the person in the berth above or below is
not, however, and is much more disturbing than
the noise of the train.   Forgetting the number
of one's berth and blundering into the wrong
place is a serious breach of good manners in a
sleeping car, and it is extremely severe on timid
persons who have gone to bed with visions before
their minds of the man who was murdered in
lower ten and the woman who brought her husband's corpse from Florida in the same berth
with her.

Among men, "picking up" acquaintances on a
train or boat is allowable if it comes about in a
natural way, but there are men who object to it.
Many business men do not discontinue their
work because they are traveling.   Portable
typewriters, secretaries, the telegraph and other
means of swift communication have made it possible for them to accomplish almost as much as
if they were in the office back home.   Such men

do not like to be interrupted, and if a garrulous or an intrusive person approaches it is within the bounds of courtesy to turn him aside. Generally, however, there is a comradery of the road, a sort of good fellowship among voyagers which lets down ordinary bars, and the men who like to rest as they travel find it highly diverting and interesting to talk with other men from various parts of the country. This holds true in hotels, especially in the commercial hotels, where traveling men foregather to meet their customers and transact their business, and in hotels in small places where the possibilities for amusement are limited and the people have to depend on one another for entertainment. But there are limits. No man should ever thrust himself upon another and it is almost an iron clad rule that he should never "pick up" women acquaintances when traveling. It is permissible to talk with them, but not to annoy them with personal attentions nor to place them under obligation by paying their bills. If a man and a woman who are traveling on the same train fall into conversation and go into the dining car together, each one should pay his or her own check, or if he insists upon paying at the table she should insist upon settling afterwards. In hotels also this is essentially true.

Hotels are judged more by the people who come to them than by anything else. The guests indicate the quality of the service, and for this reason, most hotels prefer that they be gentlemen. There is an atmosphere about a first-class hotel that frightens away second-rate people. Most places have standards and many a man has been turned away even when there was an empty room because the management did not like his looks.

Tipping is one of the most vexatious petty problems with which a traveler is confronted. It is an undemocratic custom which every sensible man deplores but sees no way around. Waiters, porters, and other functionaries who are in positions to receive tips draw very small salaries, if any. They depend upon the generosity of the public they serve. The system may be all wrong (we believe it is) but it means bread and butter to those who live by it, and it is only just, as matters are now arranged, for the traveler to pay. It is foolish to tip extravagantly or to tip every pirate who performs even the most trifling service, but a small fee, especially if the service has been good, is a courtesy not to be forgotten.

Tipping originally grew out of kindness. The knight who had received special attention at the hands of his squire expressed his gratitude by a special reward. The word "gratuity" itself indicates that the little gift was once simply a spontaneous act of thoughtfulness. It has degenerated into a perfunctory habit, but it should not be so. Excellent service deserves a recompense just as slip-shod service does not. And no one has a right to spoil a waiter (or any one else) by tipping him for inefficient work. In hotels and restaurants the standard fee is ten per cent. of the bill.

Regular travelling of any kind even under favorable circumstances is a great wear and tear on the disposition. Commuters who go in and out of town every day are a notoriously hag-ridden lot, and the men who go on the road are not much better. But there is one enormous difference. It is the privilege of the commuter to growl as much as he likes about the discomforts of the road and the stupidity of the men who make up the time tables, but travelling men—we are speaking of salesmen especially—can never indulge in the luxury of a grouch. One of the biggest parts of his job is to keep cheerful all the time and that in itself is no small task. (Try it and see.) A farmer can wear a frown as heavy as a summer thunder cloud and the potatoes will grow just the same; a mechanic can

swear at the automobile he is putting into shape
(a very impolite thing to do even when there is
no one but the machine to hear), and the bolts
and screws will hold just as fast; a lawyer can
knit his brows over his brief case and come to his
solution just as quickly as if he sat grinning at
it, but the salesman must smile, smile, smile. The
season may be dull, the crops may be bad, there
may be strikes, lockouts, depressions and defla-
tions, unemployment—it makes no difference—
he must keep cheerful. It is the courtesy of
salesmanship, and it is this quality more than any
other that makes selling a young man's job—
we do not mean in years, but in spirit—an old
one could not stand it.

In the good old days when the country was
young and everybody, from all accounts we can
gather, was happy, salesmen in the present sense
of the term were almost unknown. There were
peddlers, characters as picturesque as gipsies, who
travelled about the country preying chiefly on
the farmers. Often they spent the night—hotel
accommodations were few and houses were far
apart—and entertained the family with lively
tales of life on the road. Next morning they
gave the children trifling presents, swindled the
farmer out of several dollars and made themselves generally agreeable. The farmer took it

all in good part and looked forward with pleasure to the next visit. The peddlers came in pairs then, like snakes, but they were for the most part welcome and there was genuine regret when they became things of the past like top-buggies and Prince Albert coats.

After the peddler came the drummer, a rough, noisy chap, as his name indicates, harmless enough, but economically not much more significant than the peddler. He stayed in the business district where he was tolerated with good-natured indulgence. He was less objectionable than the man who followed him, the agent. He was (and is) a house-to-house and office-to-office canvasser and a general nuisance. He sold everything from books to life insurance, from patent potato peelers to opera glasses. He still survives, but not in large numbers, for his work, like that of the peddler and the drummer, has been swallowed up by the salesman.

The rewards which modern salesmanship holds out to those who succeed at it are so large that the field has attracted all kinds of men, highly efficient ones who love the game for its own sake, grossly incompetent ones who, having failed at something else, have decided to try this, and adventurers who believe they see in it a chance to get rich quick. The teachers of salesmanship tell us that we are all selling something, even when there is no visible product. The worker, according to them, is selling his services just as the salesman is selling goods. It may be true, but we all could not (and it is a blessing) go out and sell things in the ordinary sense in which we use the word. Some of us have to be producers. But the salesman's work is important. We do not discredit it.

Salesmanship is built on faith. A man must believe in his product and then must make other people believe in it as firmly as he does. So devoted are some salesmen to their work that it is difficult to tell whether they consider their calling a trade, a profession, a science, or a religion. Sometimes it is all four. Sometimes it goes beyond them and becomes a kind of mesmerism in which the salesman uses a sort of hypnotic process (which is simply the result of being over-anxious to sell) to persuade the prospect that he cannot wait another day before buying the particular article that the salesman is distributing. The article may be stocks and bonds, wash cloths, soap, or hair nets. It makes no difference, but he must be filled with enthusiasm and must be able to pass it along. And this very virtue which is the foundation of successful salesmanship is likely to lead the salesman into gross rudeness.

For the man who is selling is so eager and so earnest that he forgets that the man who is buying may have his own ideas on the subject.

The first step in salesmanship is to acquire a thorough knowledge of the product. The next is to gain access to the man who is to buy it. This is not always easy. Business men have been annoyed so much by agents that they have had to erect barriers, in many instances almost impenetrable ones. It is especially difficult in big cities where the pressure is heavy, but most worth while business men have learned the value of contact with the world outside and are willing to give almost any man an interview if he can show a valid reason why he should have it. Whether he gets a second interview or not depends upon how he handled the first one.

There are may ways of getting into an office. A salesman usually stands a much better chance if he writes ahead for an appointment. It is much more courteous to ask a man when he wants to see you than to drop in on him casually and trust to luck that the time is not inopportune. Some salesmen are afraid to write because they think the knowledge of what they have to sell will prejudice the prospect against it. At the same time they feel that if they can only get a chance to talk to him a few minutes

they can over-ride the prejudice. A salesman
may come into an office without letting the man
know what his purpose is (though it is best to
begin with cards on the table) but he will not
come in (unless he is a crook) under false pre-
tenses.

The friends of a salesman can sometimes be
very useful to him in presenting him to valuable
prospects, and when they feel that the meeting
will result in mutual benefit they are glad to do
it.   Sometimes the friend will give a letter or
a card of introduction.   Sometimes he will telephone or speak for an appointment.   It is best
when these come unsolicited, though it is permissible to ask for them.   No man should depend
upon the help of his friends.   A salesman should
be able to stand on his own feet, and if he and his
product together do not form a strong enough
combination to break down all obstructions there
is something wrong with one or the other of
them.

The best card of admission at the door of a
business office is a pleasing personal appearance
coupled with a calm and assured manner. This
is a universal standard of measuring a man's
character and calibre.   Until we have heard him
speak we judge him by the way he looks.   It is
a dangerous practice, as the proverb warns us,

but the percentage of hits is high enough to make us continue to use it.

A favorite device with a certain cheap type of salesman is to give his name to the girl at the entrance desk and ask her to tell Mr. Brown that Mr. Green has sent Mr. Smith to call.   The Mr. Green is entirely fictitious, but since Mr. Brown has several business acquaintances of that name, he interrupts his work and comes out to see Mr. Smith and discovers that he is a life insurance agent who thinks that if he can once get inside he can "put it across."   Most business men have no use for such practices and rarely allow the salesmen who employ them to stay in their offices any longer than it takes to get them out.   Besides, the salesman places himself under a handicap to begin with.   He will find it pretty hard to convince the man in the office that he is not dishonest about his goods just as he is about himself.   He is the greatest enemy of his profession. And he makes the work of every one else engaged in it infinitely harder.   It is something every business and profession has to fight against —the dishonest grafter who is using it as a means of swindling society.

Most salesmen give their names at the entrance desk instead of presenting their cards. Psychologists and experience have taught them

that the card is distracting and that even if the
interview is granted it is harder to get the attention of the other man if he has a card to twiddle
between his fingers.   It is more conventional to
send in a card (a good card is a letter of introduction in itself) but if the salesman finds it a
handicap, however slight, he should by all means
dispense with it.   If the card is cheap or flashy
or offensive in any way it arouses prejudice
against the man who bears it before he has had a
chance to present his case in person.   The business card may be the same as the personal card,
simply a bit of pasteboard bearing the name and
perhaps the address, or it may be larger than the
ordinary personal card and bear the name of the
firm for which the salesman is working, and in
addition, if it is a very simple design, the trademark of the firm.

Whether to rise when a caller enters and shake
hands is a question to be settled by each person
according to the way he likes best.   It is certainly more gracious to rise and ask him to be
seated before resuming one's own place.   But
promiscuous handshaking is an American habit
which Europeans as a rule frown upon and in
which a number of Americans do not indulge,
for they like the grasp of their hand to mean
something more than a careless greeting and

reserve it for their friends. In any case, the caller should not be the first to extend his hand.

If a man is accustomed to see a great number of people he will find it too much of a strain on his vitality to shake hands with them all. Roosevelt used to surprise strangers with the laxness of his grasp, but the Colonel had learned to conserve his strength in small things so that he might give it to great ones. The President of the United States has more than once in the course of the history of our country come to the end of the day with his hands bleeding from the number of times people have pressed it during the day. Now the President ought to be willing to give his life for his country, but he ought not to be required to give it in this way. It probably meant a great deal to each one of the people in the throng to be able to say, "I once shook hands with the President," but how much more it would have meant if each one of them could have said, "One day I helped my President," even if the help was so small an act of thoughtfulness as forbearing to shake his hand.

But to get back to salesmen: Some of them have a way, especially the over-zealous ones, of getting as close to the prospect as is physically possible. They place their papers or their brief cases on the desk before which the prospect is sitting, hitch their chairs up as close as they can, and talk with their breath in his face. No one likes this and it is only a rude and thoughtless salesman who is guilty of it. One man who had been vexed by it over and over again had the visitor's chair nailed to the floor in his office some little distance from his own. And he never had a caller who didn't try to move it nearer to him!

For years it has been the habit for business men to receive their callers at their desks, but lately there has been a turning away from this. The desk is usually littered with papers and letters which the caller can hardly help reading, and there are constant interruptions from the telephone and the other members of the office. For these reasons a number of business men are going out to see their callers instead of bringing them in to see them, a practice which is much more cordial than the other if one can afford the time for it. One big business house abolished its large reception room and built in a number of smaller ones instead. In this way each visitor has privacy and there is a feeling of hospitality and coziness about the little room which the bigger one failed to give. Each room was fitted up with comfortable chairs, books, and magazines so that if the caller had to wait he would have the means of entertaining himself.

Once a man agrees to see a salesman or other visitor he should give, in so far as it is possible, his full attention to him. It is better to refuse an audience altogether than to give it grudgingly. A prominent man cannot possibly see all of the people, salesmen and whatnot, who want to talk with him or he would have no time left to keep himself prominent. A busy man has to protect himself against the cranks and idlers who try to gain access to him, and most men have to have devices by which they can rid themselves of objectionable or tiresome callers. One man who has a constant stream of visitors has only one chair in his office, and he sits in it. Another never allows a visitor to enter his office, but goes to the outer reception room and stands while he talks. One man stands up as a signal that the interview is at an end. Another begins to fumble with the papers on his desk, and the salesman does not live who is not familiar with the man who must hurry out to lunch or who has only five minutes to catch a train. One man has his secretary or his office boy interrupt him after a visitor has been in as much as ten minutes, to tell him that Mr. So-and-So is waiting outside. Another rises to his feet and walks slowly toward the

door, the salesman following, until he has maneu-
vered him out. If the salesman is a man of sense
none of these devices will be necessary. He knows
that a courteous and prompt departure helps his
cause much more than an annoying persistence,
and the man who stays after his prospect's mind
has lost every interest except to get him out of
the way is lacking in one of the fundamentals of
social good manners as well as business good
manners. Rarely, perhaps never, does he succeed. For the successful salesman is the one
who can put himself into his prospect's place and
let him know that he has made a study of his
needs and is there to help him.

Carefully prepared approaches and memorized speeches are worth much to the beginner,
but an agility in adapting himself is much
more important. Ludendorff failed to get to
Paris because his original plan was upset and he
could not think quickly enough to rally the Ger-
man army and attack from a different angle.
Most salesmen have to talk to men who are con-
tinually interrupted to attend to something else.
And most business men know what they want, or
think they do, and when they ask a direct question they want a direct answer. Many a young
salesman has ruined himself so far as his career
was concerned because he went out with instruc-

tions to keep the interview in his hands and every time the man he was "selling" asked a question he passed airily over it and kept stubbornly on the road he had mapped out for himself. The salesman cannot think in theoretical terms; he must think concretely and from the point of view of the man he is trying to convince. As one very excellent salesman has put it, he must get the prospect's own story and tell it to him in different words, and if he can actually show him a way to decrease expenses or to increase output he will win not only his attention, but his heart as well.

The salesman must be absorbed in his commodity, but not to the exclusion of the man he is trying to "sell." A beginner of this type went into a man's office some time ago and rattled off a speech he had memorized about some charts. The man listened until he came to the end—the boy was talking so rapidly and excitedly that it would have been hard to interrupt him except by shouting at him—and then quietly told him that he had not been able to understand a word of what he had said. "You have not been talking to me," he explained. "You have been talking at me."

Another salesman of the same general kind went into the office of a busy lawyer one morning recently in a building which happened to be owned by the lawyer.

"I am going to give you some books," he announced.

The lawyer asked him what they were, but the salesman refused to be diverted before he had led up to the dramatic moment in his carefully planned speech at which he thought it best to mention the name of the books. He went through the whole of his canvass and then thrust a paper under the lawyer's face with "Sign here" above the dotted line.

"I thought you were going to give them to me," the lawyer said.

The salesman began to explain that of course he could not give him the books outright and so on and on and on—everybody has heard this part of his speech. The lawyer laughed and the salesman lost his temper. Very angry, he started out of the room. Near the door which opened into the hall was another door which opened into a closet that contained a shelf which was a little more than five feet high. The salesman opened this door by mistake and struck his head smartly against the shelf. This made him angrier than ever. He jerked the other door open and slammed it behind him with a crash that nearly broke the glass out. This was more than the lawyer could stand. He sprang up and started in pursuit of the salesman, who by this time was on his way into another office in the same building. The lawyer asked him where he was going. The salesman told him.

"Not in my building," the lawyer said. "I can't have the men who have offices here disturbed by people who act like this. Now go on," he added kindly but firmly, "and let's forget that you ever came here."

And the salesman went.

Salesmanship is service, and the man who persuades another to buy something he knows he does not want, does not need, and cannot use, is a scoundrel. "Good salesmanship," and this is the only sort that any self-respecting man will engage in, "is selling goods that won't come back to customers that will." It is cumulative in its effect, and the man who sells another something that really fills a want wins his eternal gratitude and friendship. He tells his friends about it, they come to the same salesman and the product begins almost to sell itself. But it takes patience and courtesy to bring it up to this point.

Some salesmen kill a territory on their first trip. Bad manners can do it very easily. Sometimes they make themselves so objectionable that the customer will buy to get rid of them, espe-

cially if the purchase does not involve more than
a dollar or two.   Sometimes they carry the customer along so smoothly with plausible arguments that they persuade him to buy something
that he knows he does not want.   It is all right
so long as the salesman is present, but discontent
follows in his trail.   Sometimes—stocks and
bonds salesmen are guilty here—they wheedle
the customer into buying more than he can afford, beginning on the premise that since their
stocks are good (and the men who sell fraudulent ones use the same methods) a man should if
he has a hundred dollars buy a hundred dollars'
worth, if he has a million he should buy a million
dollars' worth, if he has a home he must mort-
gage it, if he has an automobile he must sell it.
No good salesman works like this.   People are
very gullible and it takes little argument to persuade them to invest nearly all they have in something that will make them rich in a hurry, but the
fact that they are foolish is not quite sufficient
justification for fooling them.   Even if the
stocks and bonds are all the salesman believes
and represents them to be, no man has a right to
risk his home or his happiness for them.   A
worth while salesman leaves his customer satisfied and comes back a year later and finds him
still satisfied.   And this sort of customer is the

best advertisement and the best friend any business can have.

Bad salesmen create violent prejudices against the firms they represent. For the average customer, like the average man, judges the whole of a thing by the part that he sees. To most of us the word Chinaman calls up the picture of the laundryman around the corner in spite of the fact that there are some three hundred million Chinamen in the world engaged in other occupations. Salesmen who are consumed with their own importance do their firms more harm than good. They usually are men in positions too big for them (they may not be very big at that) and are for the most part of not much more real consequence than the gnat which sat on the tip of the bull's horn and cried, "See what a dust I raise!" Glum and sullen salesmen—there are not many of them—are of little genuine value to their firms. It is not true that when you weep you weep alone. Gloomy moods are as contagious as pleasant ones, and a happy man radiates happiness.

It is not easy to look pleasant when one's nerves are bruised from miscellaneous contacts with all sorts of people, but it is an actual fact that assuming the gestures of a mood will often induce the mood itself. The man who forces himself to *look* cheerful (we are not talking about the one who takes on an idiotic grin) may find himself after a while beginning to *feel* cheerful.   After he has greeted the elevator boy with a smile (it may be a very crooked one) and the hotel clerk and the waitress and the bootblack and the paper boy he is likely to find that the smile has straightened out into a genuine one. It does not always work—it is like counting to a hundred when one is angry—but it is worth trying.

Salesmen find their greatest difficulties among people of little education.   It is the people with fewest ideas that cling to them most tenaciously. Scholars and scientists and business men who have learned to employ scientific methods are constantly watching for something new.   They welcome new discoveries and new ideas, but the man in the backwoods of ignorance has a fence around the limits of his mind and it is hard for anything to get inside it.   He is open to conviction, but like the Scotsman, he would like to see the person who could "convict" him.   It is hard work to get a new idea into the mind of a man who is encased in a shell of ignorance or prejudice, but the salesman is worse than bad-mannered who lets another man, whoever he is, know that he thinks his religion is no good, that his political party is rotten, that his country is not worth a cancelled postage stamp, and that the people of his race are "frogs," "square-heads," "dagos," "wops," or "kikes."

Salesmen who are themselves courteous usually meet with courtesy. The people who move graciously through life find comparatively little rudeness in the world. And a good salesman is courteous to all men alike. With him overalls command as much respect as broadcloth. It pays—not only in money, but in other things that are worth more.

A salesman should be especially careful of his attitude toward the representatives of rival houses and their products. His eagerness to advance his own cause should never lead him into belittling them. He need not go out of his way to praise them nor should he speak of them insincerely in glowing terms; but an honest word of commendation shows that he is not afraid of his rivals in spite of the fact that they too have excellent goods, and when it is impossible to speak well of them it is best to stay silent.

It is not hard to see why business men spend so much time and effort in selecting their salesmen. They know that one who is ill-mannered or offensive in any way indicates either a lack of breeding or a lack of judgment on the part of the parent concern. And one is about as bad as the other.

VIII

THE BUSINESS OF WRITING

HALF the business letters which are written should never be written at all, and of the other half so many are incomplete or incoherent that a transaction which could be finished and filed away in two letters frequently requires six or eight.

A good letter is the result of clear thinking and careful planning. In the case of the sales-letter it sometimes takes several weeks to write one, but for ordinary correspondence a few minutes is usually all that is necessary. The length of time does not matter—it is the sort of letter which is produced at the end of it.

Books of commercial correspondence give a number of rules and standards by which a letter can be measured. But all rules of thumb are dangerous, and there are only two items which are essential. The others are valuable only as they contribute to them. The letter must succeed in getting its idea across and it must build up good will for its firm. And the best one is the one which accomplishes this most courteously and most completely in the briefest space of time (and paper).

There should be a reason back of every letter if it is only to say "Thank you" to a customer. Too much of our national energy goes up in waste effort, in aimless advertising, worthless salesmanship, ineffective letter writing, and in a thousand and one other ways. A lot of it is hammered out on the typewriters transcribing perfectly useless letters to paper which might really be worth something if it were given over to a different purpose.

A good letter never attracts the mind of the reader to itself as a thing apart from its contents. Last year a publishing house sent out a hundred test letters advertising one of their books. Three answers came back, none of them ordering the book, but all three praising the letter. One was from a teacher of commercial English who declared that he was going to use it as a model in his classes, and the other two congratulated the firm on having so excellent a correspondent. The physical make-up of the letter was attractive, it was written by a college graduate and couched in clear, correct, and colorful English. And yet it was no good. No *letter and no advertisement is any good which calls attention to itself instead of the message it is trying to deliver.*

There is not much room for individuality in the make-up of a letter. Custom has standardized it, and startling variations from the conventional format indicates freakishness rather than originality. They are like that astonishing gentleman who walks up Fifth Avenue on the coldest mornings in the year, bareheaded, coatless, sockless, clad in white flannels and tennis slippers. He attracts attention, but he makes us shiver.

Plain white paper of good quality is always in good taste. Certain dull-tinted papers are not bad, but gaudy colors, flashy designs, and ornate letter heads are taboo in all high types of business. Simple headings giving explicit and useful information are best. The name and address of the firm (and "New York" or "Chicago" is not sufficient in spite of the fact that a good many places go into no more detail than this), the cable address if it has one, the telephone number and the trademark if it is an inconspicuous one (there is a difference between *conspicuous* and *distinctive*) are all that any business house needs.

Hotels are often pictured on their own stationery in a way that is anything but modest, but there is a very good reason for it. The first thing most people want to know about a hotel is what sort of looking place it is. All right, here you are. Some factories, especially those that are proud of their appearance, carry their own picture on their stationery. There is nothing to say against it, but one of the most beautiful factories in America has on its letter head only the name of the firm, the address, and a small trademark engraved in black. Sometimes a picture, in a sales letter, for instance, supplements the written matter in a most effective way. And whenever any kind of device is really helpful it should by all means be used, subject only to the limits of good taste.

It is more practical in business to use standard size envelopes. If window envelopes are used the window should be clear, the paper white or nearly so, and the typewritten address a good honest black. The enclosure should fit snugly and should be placed so that the address is in plain view without having to be jiggled around in the envelope first. A letter passes through the hands of several postal clerks before it reaches the person to whom it is addressed, and if each one of them has to stop to play with it awhile an appreciable amount of time is lost, not to mention the strain it puts on their respective tempers. The paper of which an envelope is made should always be opaque enough to conceal the contents of the letter.

Practically all business letters are type-written. Occasionally a "Help Wanted" adver-tisement requests that the answer be in the appli-cant's own handwriting, but even this is rare. In most places the typing is taken care of by girls who have been trained for the purpose, but most young girls just entering business are highly irresponsible, and it is necessary for the men and women who dictate the letters to know what constitutes a pleasing make-up so that they can point out the flaws and give suggestions for doing away with them.

The letter should be arranged symmetrically on the page with ample margins all around. Noth-ing but experience in copying her own notes will teach a stenographer to estimate them correctly so that she will not have to rewrite badly placed letters. It is a little point, but an important one.

Each subject considered in a letter should be treated in a separate paragraph, and each para-graph should be set off from the others by a wider space than that between the lines, double space between the paragraphs when there is single space between the lines, triple space be-tween the paragraphs when there is a double space between the lines, and so on.

A business letter should handle only one subject. Two letters should be dispatched if two subjects are to be covered. This enables the house receiving the letter to file it so that it can be found when it is needed.

When a letter is addressed to an individual it is better to begin "Dear Mr. Brown" or "My dear Mr. Brown" than "Dear Sir" or "My dear Sir." "Gentlemen" or "Ladies" is sometime used in salutation when a letter is addressed to a group. "Dear Friend" is permissible in general letters sent out to persons of both sexes. Honorary titles should be used in the address when they take the place of "Mr.," such titles as Reverend, Doctor, Honorable (abbreviated to Rev., Dr., Hon.,) and the like. Titles should not be dropped except in the case of personal letters.

Special care should be taken with the outside address. State abbreviations should be used sparingly when there is a chance of confusion as in the case of Ga., Va., La., and Pa. "City" is not sufficient and should never be used. Nor should the name of the state ever be omitted even when the letter is addressed to some other point in the same state, as from New York to Brooklyn. And postage should be complete. A letter on which there is two cents due has placed itself under a pretty severe handicap before it is opened.

It is astonishing how many letters go out every day unsigned, lacking enclosures, carrying the wrong addresses, bearing insufficient postage, and showing other evidences of carelessness and thoughtlessness. In a town in New England last year one of the specialty shops received at Christmas time twenty different lots of money— money orders, stamps, and cash—by mail, not one of which bore the slightest clue to the identity of the sender. Countless times during the year this happens in every mail order house.

The initials of the dictator and of the stenographer in the lower left-hand corner of a letter serve not only to identify the carbon, but often to place the letter itself if it has gone out without signature. The signature should be legible, or if the one who writes it enjoys making flourishes he may do so if he will have the name neatly typed either just below the name or just above it. It should be written in ink (black or blue ink), not in pencil or colored crayon, and it should be blotted before the page is folded. The dictator himself should sign the letter whenever possible. "Dictated but not read" bears the mark of discourtesy and sometimes brings back a letter with "Received but not read" written across it. When it is necessary to leave the office before signing his letters, a business man should deputize his stenographer to do it, in which case she writes his name in full with her initials just below it. A better plan is to have another person take care of the entire letter, beginning it something like, "Since Mr. Blake is away from the office to-day he has asked me to let you know——"

The complimentary close to a business letter should be "Yours truly," "Yours sincerely" or something of the kind, and not "Yours cordially," "Yours faithfully" or "Yours gratefully" unless the circumstances warrant it.

In writing a letter as a part of a large organization one should use "We" instead of "I." A firm acts collectively, no one except the president has a right to the pronoun of the first person, and he (if he is wise) seldom avails himself of it. If the matter is so near personal as to make "We" somewhat ridiculous "I" should, of course, be used instead. But one should be consistent. If "I" is used at the beginning it should be continued throughout.

Similarly a letter should be addressed to a firm rather than to a person, for if the person happens to be absent some one else can then take charge of it. But the address should also include the name of the addressee (whenever possible) or "Advertising Manager," "Personnel Manager" or whatever the designation of his position may be. The name may be placed in the lower left-hand corner of the letter "Attention Mr. Green" or "Attention Advertising Manager," and it may also be placed just above the salutation inside the letter. Sometimes the subject of the letter is indicated in the same way, *Re Montana shipment, Re Smythe manuscript,* etc. These lines may be typed in red or in capital letters so as to catch the attention of the reader at once. If a letter is more than two pages long this line is often added to the succeeding pages, a very convenient device, for letters are sometimes misplaced in the files and this helps to locate them.

A business letter should never be longer than necessary. If three lines are enough it is absurd to use more, especially if the letter is going to a firm which handles a big correspondence. Some one has said with more truth than exaggeration that no man south of Fourteenth Street in New York reads a letter more than three lines long. But there is danger that the too brief letter will sound brusque. Mail order houses which serve the small towns and the rural districts say that, all other things being equal, it is the long sales letter which brings in the best results. Farmers have more leisure and they are quite willing to read long letters *if* (and this *if* is worth taking note of) they are interesting.

All unnecessary words and all stilted phrases should be stripped from a letter. "Replying to your esteemed favor," "Yours of the 11th inst. to hand, contents noted," "Yours of the 24th ult. received. In reply would say," "Awaiting a favorable reply," "We beg to remain" are dead weights. "Prox" might be added to the list, and "In reply to same." "Per diem" and other Latin expressions should likewise be thrown into the discard. "As per our agreement of the 17th" should give place to "According to our agreement of the 17th," and, wherever possible, simplified expression should be employed. Legal phraseology should be restricted to the profession to which it belongs. Wills, deeds, and other documents likely to be haled into court need "whereas's" and "wherefores" and "said's" and "same's" without end, but ordinary business letters do not. It is perfectly possible to express oneself clearly in the language of conversation (which is also the language of business) without burying the meaning in tiresome verbiage. And yet reputable business houses every day send out letters which are almost ridiculous because of the stiff and pompous way they are written.

The following letter was sent recently by one of the oldest furniture houses in America:

DEAR MADAM:
Herewith please find receipt for full payment of your bill.   Please accept our thanks for same.

Relative to the commission due Mrs. Robinson would say that if she will call at our office at her convenience we shall be glad to pay same to her.

Thanking you for past favors, we beg to remain,
                    Yours very truly,

Contrast that with this:

DEAR MRS. BROWN:
We are returning herewith your receipted bill.   Thank you very much.

If you will have Mrs. Robinson call at our office at her convenience we shall take pleasure in paying her the commission due her.
                    Yours very truly,

Here is another letter so typical of the kind that carelessness produces:

DEAR SIR:
I have your letter of the 27th inst. and I have forwarded it to Mr. Stubbs and will see him in a few days and talk the matter over.
                I remain
                    Yours sincerely,

Would it not have been just as easy to write:

DEAR MR. THOMPSON:
Thank you for your letter of the 27th. I have forwarded it to Mr. Stubbs and will see him in a few days to talk the matter over.
Your sincerely,

In the preparation of this volume a letter of inquiry was sent out to a number of representative business houses all over the country. It was a pleasure to read the excellent replies that came in response to it. One letter reached its destination in the midst of a strike, but the publicity manager of the firm sent a cordial answer, which began:

Your very courteous letter to Mr. Jennings came at a time when his mind is pretty well occupied with thoughts concerning the employment situation in our various plants.
We shall endeavor, therefore, to give you such information as comes to mind with regard to matters undertaken by the company which have contributed to the standard of courtesy which exists in the departments here.

We select another at random:

It pleases us very much to know that our company has been described to you as one which practises courtesy in business. We should like nothing better than to have all our employees live up to the reputation credited to them by Mr. Haight.
As for our methods of obtaining it——

Contrast these two excellent beginnings with (and this one is authentic, too) :

In reply to yours of the 6th inst. relative to what part courtesy plays in business and office management would say that it is very important.

Routine letters must be standardized—a house must conserve its own time as well as that of its customers—but a routine letter must never be used unless it adequately covers the situation. There is no excuse for a poor routine letter, for there is plenty of time to think it out, and there is no excuse for sending a routine letter when it does not thoroughly answer the correspondent's question. The man who is answering a letter must put himself in the place of the one who wrote it.

This is a fair sample of what happens when a letter is written by a person who either has no imagination at all, or does not use what he has. A woman who had just moved to New York lost the key to her apartment and wrote to her landlord for another. This answer came:

Replying to your letter, will say am sorry but it is not the custom of the landlord to furnish more than one key for an apartment. Should the tenant lose or misplace the key it is up to them to replace same.

The woman felt a justifiable sense of irritation. She was new to the city and thought she was taking the most direct method of replacing "same." Perhaps she should have known better, but she did not. Buying a key is not so simple as buying a box of matches and to a newcomer it is a matter of some little difficulty. She was at least entitled to a bit more information and to more courteous treatment than is shown in the letter signed by his landlordly hand. She went to see him and found him most suave and polite (which was his habit face to face with a woman). He explained the heavy expense of furnishing careless tenants with new keys (which she understood perfectly to begin with) and was most apologetic when he discovered that she had intended all the time to pay for it. It would have been just as easy for him in the beginning to write:

I am sorry that I cannot send you a key, but we have had so many similar requests that we have had to discontinue complying with them.

You will find an excellent locksmith at 45 West 119 St. His telephone number is Main 3480.

Or:

I am sending you the key herewith. There is a nominal charge for it which will be added to your bill at the end of the month.   I hope it will reach you safely.   It is a nuisance to be without one.

Imagination is indispensable to good letter writing, but it is going rather far when one sends thanks in advance for a favor which he expects to be conferred.   Even those who take pleasure in granting favors like to feel that they do so of their own free will.   It takes away the pleasure of doing it when some one asks a favor and then assumes the thing done.   Royalty alone are so highly privileged as to have simply to voice their wishes to have them complied with, and royalty has gone out of fashion.

At one point in their journey all the travellers in "Pilgrim's Progress" exchanged burdens, but they did not go far before each one begged to have back his original load.   That is what would happen if the man who dictates a letter were to exchange places with his stenographer. Each would then appreciate the position of the other, and if they were once in a while to make the transfer in their minds (imagination in business again) they would come nearer the sympathetic understanding that is the basis of good teamwork.

The responsibility for a letter is divided between them, and it is important that the circumstances under which it is written should be favorable. The girl should be placed in a comfortable position so that she can hear without difficulty. The dictator should not smoke whether she objects to it or not. He should have in mind what he wants to say before he begins speaking, and then he should pronounce his words evenly and distinctly. He should not bang on the desk with his fist, flourish his arms in the air, talk in rhetorical rushes with long pauses between the phrases, or raise his voice to a thunderous pitch and then let it sink to a cooing murmur. These things have not the slightest effect on the typewritten page, and they make it very hard for the girl to take correct notes. No one should write a letter while he is angry, or if he writes it (and it is sometimes a relief to write a scorching letter) he should not mail it.

It is said that Roosevelt used to write very angry letters to people who deserved them, drawing liberally upon his very expressive supply of abusive words for the occasion. Each time his secretary quietly stopped the letter. Each time the Colonel came in the day after and asked if the letter had been sent. Each time the secretary said, "No, that one did not get off." And each time the Colonel exclaimed, "Good! We won't send it!" It came to be a regular part of the day's routine.

Inexperienced dictators will find it good practice to have their stenographers read back their
letters so they can recast awkward sentences and
make other improvements. It can usually be
discontinued after a while, for dictating, like
nearly everything else, becomes easier with
habit.

A considerate man will show special forbear-
ance in breaking in a new girl. Different voices
are hard to grow accustomed to, and a girl who is
perfectly capable of taking dictation from one
man will find it very difficult to follow another
until she has grown used to the sound of his voice.
It is like learning a foreign language. The pu-
pil understands his teacher, but he does not understand any one else until he has got "the hang
of it."

The training of a good stenographer does not
end when she leaves school. She should be able
not only to take down and transcribe notes
neatly and correctly. She should be able to
spell and punctuate correctly and to make the
minor changes in phrasing and diction that so
often can make a good letter of a poor one. The
most fatal disease that can overtake a stenographer (or any one else) is the habit of slavishly
following a routine.

"Many young fellows," this is from Henry

Ford, "especially those employed in offices, fall into a routine way of doing their work that eventually makes it become like a treadmill. They do not get a broad view of the entire business. Sometimes that is the fault of the employer, but that does not excuse the young man. Those who command attention are the ones who are actually pushing the boss. . . . It pays to be ahead of your immediate job, and to do more than that for which you are paid. A mere clock watcher never gets anywhere. Forget the clock and become absorbed in your job. Learn to love it."

The position of secretary is a responsible one. Frequently she knows almost as much about his business as her employer himself (and sometimes even more). He depends upon her quite as much as she depends upon him, though in a somewhat different way. It takes personal effort together with native ability to raise any one to a position of importance, but personal effort often needs supplementing, and many business houses have taken special measures to help their employees to become good correspondents.

In some places there are supervisors who give talks and discuss the actual letters, good ones and bad, which have been written. They go over the carbons and hold conferences with the correspondents who need help.   In other places courtesy campaigns for a higher standard of correspondence are held, while in others the matter is placed in the hands of the heads of the various departments, acting on the assumption that these heads are men of experience and ability or they would never have attained the position they hold.

The president of a bank which has branches in London and Paris and other big foreign cities used every now and then to stop the boy who was carrying a basket of carbons to the file clerk and look them over.   If he found a letter he did not like, or one that he did like a great deal, he sent for the person who wrote it and talked with him. It was not necessary for him to go over the letters often.   The fact that the people in the office knew that it was likely to happen kept them on the alert and nearly every letter that left the organization was better because the person who wrote it knew that the man at the head was interested in it and that there was a strong chance that he might see it.

What is effective in one place may not be so in another.   Each house must work out its own system.   But one thing must be understood in the beginning, and that is that the spirit of courtesy must first abide in the home office before the people who work there can hope to send it out through the mail.

Roughly speaking there are eight types of business letters which nearly every business man at one time or another has to write or to consider.

The first is the letter of *application*. The applicant should state simply his qualifications for the place he wants. He should not make an appeal to sympathy (sob stuff) nor should he beg or cringe. He should not demand a certain salary, though he may state what salary he would like, and he should not say "Salary no object." It would probably not be true. There are comparatively few people with whom money is no object. If it is the first time the applicant has ever tried for a position he should say so; if not, he should give his reason for leaving his last place. It should not be a long letter. A direct statement of the essential facts (age, education, experiences, etc.) is all that is necessary.

Many times the letter of application is accompanied by, or calls for, a letter of *recommendation*.

No man should allow himself to recommend another for qualities which he knows he does not possess. If he is asked for a recommendation he should speak as favorably of the person under

consideration as he honestly can, and if his opinion of him is disapproving he should give it with
reservations.

At one time during the cleaning up of Panama
there was considerable talk about displacing
General Gorgas and a committee waited on
Roosevelt to suggest another man for the job.
He listened and then asked them to get a letter
about him from Dr. William H. Welsh of Johns
Hopkins. Dr. Welsh wrote a letter praising
the man very highly, but ended by saying that
while it was true that he would be a good man for
the place, he did not think he would be as good
as the one they already had—General Gorgas.
The Colonel acted upon the letter confident
(because he had great faith in Dr. Welsh) that
he was taking the wise course, which subsequent
events proved it to be. "Would to heaven," he
said, "that every one would write such honest
letters of recommendation!"

The general letter of recommendation beginning "To whom it may concern" is rarely given
now. It has little weight. Usually a man waits
until he has applied for a position and then gives
the name of his reference, the person to whom he
is applying writes to the one to whom he has
been referred, and the entire correspondence is
carried on between these two. In this way the

letter of recommendation can be sincere, something almost impossible in the open letter. It is needless to add that all such correspondence should be confidential.

The letter of *introduction* is, in a measure, a letter of recommendation. The one who writes it stands sponsor for the one who bears it. It should make no extravagant claims for the one who is introduced. He should simply be given a chance to make good on his own responsibility. But it should give the reason for the presentation and suggest a way of following it up that will result in mutual pleasure or benefit. It should be in an unsealed envelope and the envelope should bear, in addition to the address, the words, "Introducing Mr. Blank" on the lower left-hand corner. This does away with an embarrassing moment when the letter is presented in person and enables the host to greet his guest by name and ask him to be seated while he reads it.

Letters of introduction should not be given promiscuously. Some men permit themselves to be persuaded into giving letters of introduction to people who are absolute nuisances (it is hard to refuse any one who asks for this sort of letter, but often kindest for all concerned) and then they send in secret another letter explaining how the first one came about. This really throws the burden on the person who least of all ought to bear it, the innocent man whom the first one wanted to meet. No letter of presentation is justified unless there is good reason behind it, such, as for instance, in the following:

This is Mr. Franklin B. Nesbitt. He has been in Texas for several months studying economic conditions, and I believe can give you some valuable information which has resulted from his research there. He is a man upon whom you can rely. I have known him for years, and I am sure that whatever he tells you will be trustworthy.

It is a common practice for a business man to give his personal card with "Introducing Mr. Mills" or "Introducing Mr. Mills of Howard and Powell Motor Co." written across it to a man whom he wishes to introduce to another. This enables him to get an interview. What he does with it rests entirely with him.

Sales letters are a highly specialized group given over, for the most part, to experts. Their most common fault is overstatement or patronizing. The advertisements inserted in trade papers and the letters sent out to the "trade" are often so condescendingly written that they infuriate the men to whom they are addressed. It is safer to assume that the man you are writing to is an intelligent human being. It is better to overestimate his mentality than to underestimate it, and it is better to "talk" to him in the letter than to "write" to him.

Sales letters are, as a rule, general, not personal, and yet the best ones have the personal touch. The letter is a silent salesman whose function is to anticipate the needs of its customers and offer to supply them. In this as in any other kind of salesmanship it is the spirit which counts for most, and the spirit of genuine helpfulness (mutual helpfulness) gives pulling power to almost any letter. The one which presents a special offer on special terms specially arranged for the benefit of the customer wins out almost every time, provided, of course, that the offer is worth presenting. There is no use in declaring that all of the benefit is to the subscriber. It would be very foolish if it were actually true. Once a man went into a haberdashery to buy a coat. The shop owner unctuously declared that he was not making a cent of profit, was selling it for less than it cost him, and so on and on. The man walked out. "I'll go somewhere where they have sense enough to make a profit," he said.

A sales letter should never be sent out to a large group of people without first having been tried out on a smaller one. In this way the letter can be tested and improvements made before the whole campaign is launched. The results in the small group are a pretty fair indication of what they will be in the large one, and a tremendous amount of time and money can be saved by studying the letter carefully to see where it has failed before sending it out to make an even bigger failure.

On the face of things it seems that an *order letter* would be an easy one to write, but the mail order houses have another story to tell. Order blanks should be used wherever possible. They have been carefully made and have blank spaces for the filling in of answers to the questions that are asked. In an order letter one should state exactly what he wants, how he wants it sent, and how he intends to pay for it. If the order consists of several items, each one should be listed separately. If they are ordered from a catalogue they should be identified with the catalogue description by mention of their names, their numbers and prices. One should state whether he is sending check, money, stamps, or money order, but he should not say "Enclosed please find."

The commonest form of *letter of acknowledgment* is sent in answer to an order letter. If there is to be the least delay in filling the order the letter acknowledging it should say so and should give the reason for it, but even when the order is filled promptly (if it is a large or a comparatively large one) the letter of acknowledgment should be sent.   Then if anything goes wrong it is easier to trace than when the customer has no record except the copy of his order letter.   The letter of acknowledgment should simply thank the customer and assure him of prompt and efficient service.

Complaints should be acknowledged immediately.   If there is to be a delay while an investigation is made, the letter of acknowledgment should simply state the fact and beg indulgence until it is finished.   Complaints should *always* receive careful and courteous attention. Most of them are justified, and even those that are not had something to begin on.

The *letter of complaint* should never be written hastily or angrily.   It should go directly to the root of the trouble and should state as nearly as possible when and where and how it came about.   One should be especially careful about placing the blame or charging to an individual what was really the fault of an unfortunate train of circumstances.   The tone should never be sharp, no matter how just the complaint. "Please" goes further than "Now, see here."

Collection letters are hardest to write. They should appeal to a man's sense of honor first of all. It is a cheap (and ineffective) method to beg him to pay because you need the money, and rarely brings any reaction except rousing in his mind a contempt for you. The first letter in a series (and the series often includes as many as six or eight) should be simply a reminder. Drastic measures should not be taken until they are necessary, and at no time should the letters become abrupt or insulting. In the first place, it is ungentlemanly to write such letters, in the second it antagonizes the debtor, and if he gets angry enough he feels that it is hardly an obligation to pay the money; that it will "serve 'em right" if he does not do it.

Advertising is a sort of letter writing. Each advertisement is a letter set before the public or some part of the public in the hope that it will be answered by the right person. It enters into an over-crowded field and if it is to attract attention it must be vivid, unusual, and convincing. Increasingly—and there is cause to be thankful for this—exaggerated statements are being forced to disappear. In the first place the ballyhoo advertisers have shouted the public deaf. They no longer believe. In the second place advertisers themselves have waked to the menace of

the irresponsible and dishonest people who are
advertising and are taking legal measures to
safeguard the honor of the profession.

One of the most successful advertisers of modern times was a man who carried the idea of service into everything he did.   For a while he had
charge of soliciting advertising for automobile
trucks for a certain magazine.   Instead of going
at it blindly he made a careful study of the map
of the United States and marked off the areas
where automobile trucks were used, where they
could be used, and where they should be used,
and sent it to the manufacturers along with a
statement of the circulation of the magazine and
the advantages of reaching the public through
it.   The result was that the magazine got more
advertising from the manufacturers than it could
possibly handle.   It is very gratifying to know
that this man succeeded extraordinarily as an advertiser, for not once during his long career did
he ever try to "put one over" on the public or on
anybody else.

No advertisement should be impertinent or
importunate.   During the war there was a splendid poster bearing a picture of Uncle Sam looking straight into your eyes and pointing his finger straight into your face as he said, "Young
man, your country needs you!"   The poster was

excellent from every point of view, but since the war, real estate companies, barber shops, restaurants and whatnot have used posters bearing the pictures of men pointing their fingers straight at you saying, "There is a home at Blankville for you," "Watch out to use Baker's Best," and "You're next!" After all, Uncle Sam is the only person who has a right to point his finger at you in any such manner and say, "I need you." And besides, there is the moral side of it. Imitation is the sincerest flattery, but the dividing line between it and dishonesty is not always clear. And the law cannot every time prosecute the offender, for there is a kind of cleverness that enables a man to pilfer the ideas of another and recast them just sufficiently to "get by." It would be very stupid for a man not to profit by the experience of other men, but there is a vast difference betwen intelligent adaptation of ideas and stealing them. This is more a question of morals than of manners, for the crime—and it is a crime—is usually deliberate, while most breaches of manners are unintentional and due to either carelessness or ignorance.

House memoranda are letters among the various people who are working there. They should be brief, above all things, and clear, but never at the sacrifice of courtesy. Titles should not be dropped and nicknames should not be used although initials may be. Memoranda should never be personal unless they are sent confidentially.   An open memorandum should never contain anything that cannot be read by every one without reflecting unfavorably upon any one. And it is wise to keep in mind—no matter what you are writing—that the written record is permanent.

IX

MORALS AND MANNERS

IT HAS become a habit of late years for people
to argue at great length about right and wrong,
and what with complexes and psycho-analysis
and what with this and that, they have almost
come to the conclusion that there is no right and
wrong.   Man, so they have decided, is a frail and
tender being completely at the mercy of the
traits he has inherited from his ancestors and
those he has acquired from his neighbors.   What
he does is simply the result of the combination of
circumstances that have made him what he is.
There is some truth in it, of course, but what
there is is no bigger than a mustard seed, and all
the volumes that have been written about it, all
the sermons that have been preached upon it, and
all the miles of space that have been devoted to
it in the newspapers and magazines have not
served to increase it.   Most of us never give any
one else credit for our achievements and there is
no more reason for giving them blame for our
failures.   A gentleman is "lord of his own

actions." He balances his own account, and whether there is a debit or a credit is a matter squarely up to him.

The pivot upon which all right-thinking conduct involving relations with other people turns is the Golden Rule, "Whatsoever ye would that men should do to you, do ye even so to them." It is to the moral what the sun is to the physical world, and just as we have never made full use of the heat and light which we derive from the sun but could not live without that which we do use, so we have never realized more than a small part of the possibilities of the Golden Rule, but at the same time could not get along together in the world without the meagre part of it that we do make use of. The principle is older than the Christian Era, older than the sequoias of California, older than the Pyramids, older than Chinese civilization. It is the most precious abstract truth that man has yet discovered. It contains the germ of all that has been said and written about human brotherhood and all that has been done toward making it an accomplished fact. And if to-morrow it were to vanish from the earth we should miss it almost, if not quite, as much as we should the sun if it were to go hurtling off into space so far away that we could neither see nor feel it. In the one case there would be no life at all on earth, in the other there would be none worth living.

The Golden Rule amounts to no more than putting yourself into another person's place. It is not always easy to do. Half of the people in the United States have very little idea of what the lives of the other half are like and have no special interest in knowing.

"What," we asked the manager of a bookshop which caters to a large high-grade clientèle, "do you find your greatest trouble?"

"Lack of imagination on the part of our customers," he answered promptly, "a total inability to put themselves into our place, to realize that we have our lives to live just as they have theirs. If we haven't a book in stock they want to know why. If we don't drop everything to attend to them they want to know why. If anything goes wrong they want to know why, but they won't listen to explanations and won't accept them when they do. They simply can't see our side of it. And they make such unreasonable demands. Why, last year during the Christmas rush when the shop was fairly jammed to the door and we were all in a perfect frenzy trying to wait on them all, a man called up to know if his wife was here!"

It is not always easy to see life, or even a small

section of life, from another person's point of view. A man very often thinks housework practically no work at all (the drudgery of it he has never realized because he has never had to do it) and a woman very often underestimates the wear and tear and strain of working in an office and getting a living out of it in competition with hundreds of other men. Marie Antoinette had no conception of what it meant when the French people cried for bread. It seemed impossible to her that a person could actually be hungry. "Why, give them cake!" she exclaimed. It may be pretty hard for a man who is making $10,000 a year to sympathize with the stenographer he hires for $600 or $700 a year, or for her to see his side of things. But it is not impossible.

Very few of us could honestly go as far as the novelist who recently advocated the motto: "My neighbor is perfect" or the governor who set aside a day for the people in his state to put it into practice. We happen to know that our neighbors are, like ourselves, astonishing compounds of vice and virtue in whom any number of improvements might be made. It is not necessary to think them perfect, only to remember that each one of us, each one of them, is entitled to life, liberty, and the pursuit of happiness. In other words, that every man has a right to a square deal.

In the ancient world there were four cardinal virtues: justice, prudence, temperance, and discretion. In the modern world of business there are only two. Others may follow, but these two must come first. Justice, we mean, and kindness. No man was ever really a gentleman who was not just and kind, and we think it would be almost impossible for one who is, whatever his minor shortcomings may be, not to be a gentleman. Just to his employees (or to his employer), to his customers, to his friends, to himself, and this justice always tempered with kindness, the one quality giving the firmness necessary in dealing with people, the other the gentleness which is no less necessary.

In the first place, and this is one of the corner stones of justice, industrial life must be made safe for the worker. And it is a job in which he has as large a part as the man who hires him. Under present conditions one workman out of every eight is injured during the year and the accident is as often his fault as it is that of his employer. In some instances efficient safety devices are not provided, in others they are not made use of.

Special kinds of work, such as that in which the

laborer is exposed to poisonous fumes, to sand blasts, dangerous chemicals or mineral dusts, need special protective devices and men with sense enough to use them. The employer cannot do his share unless the worker does his, and the worker is too quick to take a chance. The apprentice is usually cautious enough, but the old hand grows unwary. Ninety-nine times he thrusts his arm in among belts whirling at lightning speed and escapes, but the hundredth time the arm is caught and mangled. And there is nothing to blame but his own carelessness.

WHO AM I?

I am more powerful than the combined armies of the world.

I have destroyed more men than all the wars of the nations.

I am more deadly than bullets, and I have wrecked more homes than the mightiest of siege guns.

I steal, in the United States, alone, over $300,000,000 each year.

I spare no one, and I find my victims among the rich and poor alike, the young and old, the strong and weak. Widows and orphans know me.

I loom up to such proportions that I cast my shadow over every field of labor, from the turning of the grindstone to the moving of every railroad train.

I massacre thousands upon thousands of wage earners a year.

I lurk in unseen places and do most of my work silently. You are warned against me but you heed not.

I am relentless.

I am everywhere—in the house, on the streets, in the factory, at the railroad crossings, and on the sea.

I bring sickness, degradation and death, and yet few seek to avoid me.

I destroy, crush or maim; I give nothing but take all.

I am your worst enemy.

I AM CARELESSNESS

Any kind of carelessness which results in injury (or is likely to result in it), whether the injury is mental or physical, is criminal. No plea can justify building a theatre which cannot stand a snowstorm, a school which cannot give a maximum of safety to the children who are in it, a factory which does not provide comfortable working conditions for the people employed there, or allowing any unsafe building or part of a building to stand.

There is a factory (this story is true) which places the lives of the majority of its employees in jeopardy twice a day.   There are two sets of elevators, one at the front of the building for the executives and their secretaries and visitors, one at the rear for the rank and file of the employees.   Since there are several hundred of the latter the advantages of the division are too obvious to need discussion.   We have no quarrel with it.   But the apparatus upon which the elevators in the rear run is so old and so rotten and so rusty that there is constant danger of its breaking down.   Three times already there have been serious accidents.   The men who are hired to operate the cars rarely stay more than a week or so.   Protests have been sent in but nothing has been done.   The management knows what the conditions are but they have never stopped to realize the horror of it.   It is not that they value a few dollars more than they do human life, but that they simply do not stop to think or to imagine what it would be like to have to ride in the ramshackle elevator themselves.   In the offices of this factory there is an atmosphere of courtesy and good breeding far beyond the ordinary—in justice to the people there it must be said that they do not know the conditions in the rear, but the management does.   And the management is polite in most of its dealings, both with its employees and outside, but polish laid over a cancerous growth like this is not courtesy.

There are three essentials for good work: *good lighting* (it must be remembered that a light that is too glaring is as bad as one that is too dim), *fresh air* (air that is hot and damp or dry and dusty is not fresh), and *cleanliness* (clean workrooms—and workers—clean drinking water with individual drinking cups, and in places where the work is unusually dirty, plenty of clean water for bathing purposes.)

In the matter of salaries—economically one of the most important questions in the world—the employer should pay, not as little, but as much as he can afford. No man has a right to hire a girl (or a boy either) at less than a living wage and expect her to live on it. The pitiless publicity which was given the evil of hiring girls at starvation wages some years ago (in particular through the short stories of O. Henry, "the little shop-girl's knight" which, according to Colonel Roosevelt, suggested all the reforms which he undertook in behalf of the working girls of New York) did much in the way of reform, but there is much yet to be done.

Money has been called the root of all evil. It is not money, but greed. Greed and thought-

lessness. Sir James Barrie says stupidity and
jealousy, but both these might be included under
thoughtlessness. Men who are generous almost
to a fault when a case of individual need is
brought before them will hire girls at less than
any one could exist on in decency. When they
meet these same girls in the hall or when they
come directly into contact with them in their
work they may be polite enough, but their politeness is not worth a tinker's curse. Justice must
come first. Only if the employer pays a fair
day's wage can he expect a fair day's work.
"Even then," he protests, "I can't get it." And
this is, unfortunately, in large measure true. As
Kipling said some few years ago, and it still
holds,

> From forge and farm and mine and bench
>   Deck, altar, outpost lone—
> Mill, school, battalion, counter, trench,
>   Rail, senate, sheepfold, throne—
> Creation's cry goes up on high
>   From age to cheated age:
> "Send us the men who do the work
>   For which they draw the wage."

"I can't even get them here on time," the employer's wail continues. The employee may
respond that the employer is not there, but this
has nothing to do with it. Most people are paid

to get to their work at a certain hour.   They have a daily appointment with their business at a specified time.   It is wise and honorable to keep it.   Tardiness is a habit, and, like most others, considerably harder to break than to form, but punctuality also is a habit, not quite so easy to establish as tardiness because it is based on strength while the other is based on weakness.   Most of us hate to get up in the morning, but it is good discipline for the soul, and we have the words of poets as well as of business men that

> Early to bed and early to rise
> Is the way to be healthy, wealthy, and wise.

Time is one of the most valuable of commodities.   More people are discharged for coming in late than for any other reason, not excepting (we believe this no exaggeration) "lay-offs" during dull seasons.   Slipping out before the regular time and soldiering on the job fall into the same classification with tardiness.   Such practices the employee too often looks upon as a smart way of getting around authority, blithely ignoring the fact which has so many times been called to our attention: that what a man does to a job is not half so important as what the job does to him.

The material loss which comes from it is the least of its harms.

All work and no play makes Jack a dull boy, but he is duller yet if he tries to mix them. Intense concentration during working hours followed by complete rest is the only way to make a contented workman, and it is the happy workman (just as it is the happy warrior), in spite of all that is said about divine discontent, who counts for most both to himself and to his community. There is a gladness about earnest eager work which is hard to find in anything else. "I know what pleasure is," declared Robert Louis Stevenson, "because I have done good work."

Gossiping, idling, smoking, writing personal letters during working hours (these usually on the firm's stationery), and a thousand and one other petty acts of dishonesty are ruinous, not so much to the house which tolerates them (because it cannot help itself) as to the person who commits them. Telephones are the cause of a good deal of disturbance during business hours in places where employees spend an appreciable amount of time on personal calls. In some organizations they are prohibited altogether; but in most they are allowed if not carried to excess. It is not business people who need education in this so much as their friends who have never been in business and seem unable to realize that personal calls are not only annoying, but time-killing and distracting.

Part of the unrest and unhappiness among employees is due to the fact that vast numbers of them are working not at what they want to do but at what they have to do, marking time until they can get something better. It is very commendable for a man to be constantly watching out to improve himself, but it does not in the meanwhile excuse him from doing his best at the job for which he is drawing pay. It is dishonest. It is unsportsmanlike. It is unmanly.

The question of salary is, from whatever angle it is approached, a delicate one. "My experience is," observed David Harum, "that most men's hearts is located ruther closter to their britchis pockets than they are to their vest pockets." It is a tender subject, and one that causes more trouble than almost any other in the world. Employees who are trusted with the payroll should not divulge figures and employees who are on the payroll should not discuss and compare salaries. Jones cannot understand why Brown gets more than he does when he knows that Brown's work is not so good, Brown cannot see why Smith gets as much as he does when he is out two or three days in the week, and Smith cannot see why he has not been made an executive after all the years he has worked in the place. There are many sides to the matter of salary adjustment and they all have to be taken into consideration. And the petty jealousies that employees arouse by matching salaries against one another only serve to make a complex problem more difficult.

There is only one base upon which a man should rest his plea for an increase in salary, and that is good work. The fact that he has a family dependent upon him, that he is ill or hard up may be ample reason for giving him financial help or offering him a loan, but it is no reason why his salary should be increased unless his work deserves it. Paternalism is more unfair than most systems of reward, and the man who comes whimpering with a tale of hard luck is usually (but not always) not worth coddling. Years of experience, even though they stretch out to three score and ten, are not in themselves sufficient argument for promotion. Sometimes the mere fact that a man has been content to stay in one place year after year shows that he has too little initiative to rise in that particular kind of work and is too timid to try something else.

Another big cause of trouble among men

working in the same organization is rigid class distinction. When a man hires others to work *for* him he invites discontent; when he hires them to work *with* him there may be dissatisfaction, but the chances of it are lessened. A business well knit together is like any other group, an army or a football team, bound into a unit to achieve a result. At its best each person in it feels a responsibility toward each one of the others; each realizes that who a man is is not half so important as what he does, and that

> . . . the game is more than the player of the game
> And the ship is more than the crew,

or, as another poet with a Kiplingesque turn of mind and phrase has it,

> It is not the guns or armament
> Or the money they can pay.
> It's the close coöperation
> That makes them win the day.
> It is not the individual
> Or the army as a whole,
> But the everlastin' team work
> Of every blooming soul.

Each man is directly responsible to his immediate superior. He should never, unless the circumstances are unusual, go over his head and he should never do so without letting him know.

It should be impossible, and is, in a well-organized house, for men coming from the outside to appeal over a member of a firm. Responsible men should be placed in the contact positions and their responsibility should be respected. Salesmen are warned not to bother with the little fellow but to go straight to the head of a firm. Like most general advice, it is dangerous to put into universal practice. The heads of most firms have men to take care of visitors, and in a good many instances, the salesman helps his cause by going to the proper subordinate in the first place. It is all very well to go to the head of a firm but to do it at the expense of the dignity of one of the smaller executives is doubtful business policy and doubtful ethics.

"Passing the buck" is a gentle vice practised in certain loosely hung together concerns. It is a strong temptation to shift the accountability for a mistake to the shoulders of the person on the step below, but it is to be remembered that temptations, like obstacles, are things to be overcome. "The "buck," as has been pointed out, always passes down and not up, a fact which makes a detestable practice all the more odious. One of the first laws of knighthood was to defend the weak and to protect the poor and helpless; it still holds, though knighthood has passed out of existence; and the creature (he is not even good red herring) who blames some one else for a fault of his, or allows him to take the blame, is beneath contempt.

When a mistake has been made and the responsibility fixed on the right person the penalty may be inflicted. If it is a scolding or a "bawling out" it should be done quietly. Good managers do not shout their reprimands. They do not need to. The reproof for a fault is a matter between the offender and the "boss." No one else has any concern with it, and there is no reason why the instinct for gossip or the appetite for malicious reports on the part of the other employees should be satisfied. The world would be happier and business would be infinitely more harmonious if each person in it could realize that his chief aim in life should be to mind his own business or, at least, to let other people's alone.

Private secretaries and other people in more or less confidential positions are many times tempted to give away secret information, not so much for the benefit of the person to whom it is given as to show how much they themselves are trusted. Nearly every one who holds a responsible business position receives items of information which are best not repeated, and if common sense does not teach him what should be kept private and what should be told, nothing will. It should not be necessary for the superior to preface each of his remarks with, "Now, this must go no further."

Matters concerning salaries should always be confidential, and so should personal items such as health reports, character references, and so on, credit reports, blacklists, and other information of a similar nature. It is compiled for a definite purpose and for the use of a limited group of people. It is unethical to use it in any other way.

The reason for dismissing a person from a business organization should be kept private, especially if it is something that reflects unfavorably on his character. But the reason should *always* be given to the employee himself. He may not listen, and most of the men who have had experience in hiring and firing say that he will not, but that is his own responsibility. The employer has no right to let him go without letting him know why. And the employee should listen—it may not be his fault but he should check up honestly with himself and find out. The same thing that lost him this place may lose him another, and a good many times all that he can get out of being discharged is a purification of soul. It is a pity if he misses that.

Discharging a person is a serious matter, serious from both sides, and it is not a thing to be done lightly. Most houses try to obviate it in so far as possible by hiring only the kind of people they want to keep. "Our efforts toward efficiency" (we quote from one manager who is typical of thousands) "begin at the front door. We try to eliminate the unfit there. We do not employ any one who happens to come along. We try by means of an interview and references and psychological tests to get the very highest type of employee." No human test is perfect, however, and there are times, even in the best regulated houses, when it becomes necessary to dismiss persons who have shown themselves unfit.

It is not always a disgrace to be discharged and it is not always a step downward. It may be because of business depression or it may be because the man is a square peg in a round hole. Sometimes it is the only experience that will reduce a man's, especially a young man's, idea of his own importance to something like normal proportions, the only one that will clear his mind of the delusion that he is himself the only person who is keeping off the rocks the business for which he is working, in which case it is one of the best things that could have happened to him.

A roll call of famous or successful men who

were fired would take up several reams of paper, and it is a pretty rash personnel manager (not to say brutal and unfair) who will throw a man out like a rotten potato and declare that he is absolutely no good. Besides, he does not know. All that he can be sure of is that the man was not qualified for the job he was holding. And he should think twice before giving a man a bad name even if he feels certain that he deserves it. At the same time he must protect himself and other business men from incompetent, weak, or vicious employees. If after his dismissal a man sends back to his former employer for a recommendation, the recommendation should be as favorable as possible without sacrificing the truth.

When a man breaks his connection with a business house, whether he does so voluntarily or involuntarily, his departure should be pleasant, or at the least dignified. It is childish to take advantage of the fact that you are going away to tell all of the people you have grudges against how you feel about them, and it is worse than a mere breach of good manners to abuse the house that has asked you to leave. If it has done some one else an injustice, talk about that all you please, but on your own account be silent. Even if the fault has been altogether

with the house it does not help to call it names.
Self-respect should come to the rescue here. This
is the time when it is right to be too proud to
fight.

For a long time it has been held bad ethics for
the members of one trade or profession to speak
disparagingly of their competitors, and we have
grown accustomed to say that you can judge a
man by the way he speaks of his rivals.   This
has limits, however, and in some instances a mis-
taken idea of loyalty to one's calling has led to
the glossing over of certain evils which could
have been cured much earlier if they had been
made public.   It is all very well to be generous
and courteous toward one's competitors but the
finest courtesy in any business consists of doing
whatever tends to elevate the standard of that
business.

Every man likes his business to be well thought
of, and most businesses have organized for
the promotion of a high standard of ethics
as well as for the development of more efficient
methods.   Notable among these, to mention one
of the most recent ones, is the Advertisers' Association.   There was a time when the whole profession was menaced by the swindlers who were
exploiting fraudulent schemes by means of
advertising in magazines and newspapers, but

to-day no reputable periodical will accept an advertisement without investigating its source and most of them will back up the guarantee of the advertiser that his goods are what he represents them to be with a guarantee of their own. No publication which intends to keep alive can afford a reputation of dishonesty, and the efforts of the publishers toward cleaning up have been seconded by the association to such an extent that any person or corporation that issues a deceptive advertisement, whether or not there was intent to deceive, will be prosecuted and punished.

There was a time when a man could do almost anything within the law in a commercial transaction and excuse himself by saying "business is business." Happily this is no longer true. Business men have not grown perfect but they have raised their standards of business morality as high as their standards of personal morality. They have learned that business and life are one, that our lives cannot—and this has a number of disadvantages—be separated into compartments like so many tightly corked bottles on a shelf. We have only one vessel and whatever goes into it colors what is already there. And it is significant to remember that muddy water poured into clean water will make it muddy, but that clean water poured into muddy water will not

make it clean. It takes very little ink in a pail
of milk to color the whole of it, but it takes an
enormous amount of milk to have any effect on
a bottle of ink.

Business men have also learned that the only
way to build a business that will last is to lay its
foundation on the Golden Rule, and many a man
who might otherwise sidetrack the principles of
integrity holds by them for this reason. "Honesty," declared one of the most insufferable prigs
America ever produced, "is the best policy." He
was right. Prigs usually are. It is only because they are so sure of it themselves that they
irritate us.

It is a fact, in spite of the difficulty Diogenes
had when he took up his lantern and set out to
find an honest man, that most people like to pay
their way as they go, and the business men who
recognize this are the ones who come out on top.
They do not say that the customer is always right
nor that he is perfect, but they assume that he is
honest and trust him until he has proved himself
otherwise. The biggest mail order house in
America never questions a check. As soon as
an order is received they fill it and attend to the
check afterward. Their percentage of loss is
extraordinarily small. Distrust begets distrust,
and the perversity of human nature is such that

even an honest man will be tempted to cheat if he knows another suspects him of it. The converse is equally true. There are, of course, exceptions. But the only rule in the world to which there are no exceptions is that there is no rule that holds good under all conditions.

PART II

X

"BIG BUSINESS"

IN THE preceding pages we have looked over the field of etiquette in business in a general way, and have come to the only conclusion possible, namely, that the basis of courtesy in business is common sense, and that whatever rules may be given must not be followed slavishly, but must simply be used as guide posts. In the pages which follow we shall go into detail and watch courtesy at work among certain groups and individuals.

Let us take, for example, a big concern which employs a thousand or more people. We shall begin with the president.

President of a Big Organization. Here is a man who bears a heavy responsibility. He has not only his own welfare to look after but that of the men and women who work *with* (we like this word better than *for*) him. His first duty is to them. How can he best perform it?

It is a matter of fact that few men rise to such positions who are not innately courteous. It is

one of the qualities which enable them to rise.
For this reason we shall take it for granted that
the president needs no instructions. Already he
has learned the great value of courtesy. But
this does not protect him always from discourtesy in other people.

Every man who holds a high position in a big
organization is besieged with visitors, but no one
so much as the president. He is a target for
cranks and idlers and freaks as well as for earnest business men who want to help him or to get
help from him. Thousands during the course of
a year come to call on him. If he saw them all
he would have to turn over the presidency to
some one else and devote himself to entertaining
visitors. Many of those who come ask for him
when he is not at all the man they want to see,
but they have been taught in the schools of salesmanship or they have read in a magazine that it
never pays to bother with the little fellow, but
that they should go straight to the top.

Every minute of the time of the president
of a big company is valuable (all time is valuable, as far as that goes), and it must be pro-
tected from the people who have no right to in-
fringe upon it.

You would think that the vice-presidents and
the managers and the various executives would

be his best protection. They are not. It is the person who is placed at the front door to receive visitors. We shall consider him next.

The Man at the Door. As a matter of fact, this person is usually a girl, many times a very young and irresponsible one, because great numbers of business men have not yet realized the importance of the position. A well-poised girl or a woman who has had wide experience in handling people can fill the place quite as efficiently as a man, and a great deal more so if the man has not been chosen because he has the quick sympathy and ready tact so necessary in taking care of the needs of a miscellaneous assortment of callers.

In the house we are observing the person at the door is a young man who began as a messenger boy, and who, because he did what he was asked to do cheerfully instead of sullenly, with a "Certainly, sir," and a smile instead of a "That's Bob's business" and a frown, was made manager of the messengers, and then first assistant of the man at the door, and later, when that man was given another position, was promoted to his place. The job commands a good salary and offers chances of promotion. The young man likes it.

A visitor comes, a young salesman, let us say,

who has had little experience. This is only the second or third time he has tried to storm the doors of big business. He asks at once for the president. He does not give his card because the school where he learned his trade cautioned him against doing so. (He is perfectly correct, and he would have been equally correct if he had given it. The more formal style is to send in the card.) The man at the door sees at once what kind of man he has to deal with.

"The president is busy," he answers—a safe re-mark always, because if he is not he should be; "maybe I can do something for you."

The salesman explains that he has an attach-ment to increase efficiency of typewriters. He would like to show the president how it works.

"Oh, you don't want Mr. President," the host answers. "You want Mr. Jones. He attends to all such things for us. Will you be seated here in the reception room," motioning toward the door which is at one side of his desk, "while I find out if he is busy?"

This concern is very conservative about buying new attachments and new machinery of any kind, but it is ever on the alert to discover means of in-creasing its output and saving its manpower. Almost any new idea is worth a demonstration.

If the man at the desk has an intelligent messenger boy—and he should have—he sends him in to Mr. Jones. The boy finds Mr. Jones busy. He will be free in about fifteen minutes and then will be glad to see the salesman. The man reports to the visitor and asks if he cares to wait. He does. The host offers him a magazine and asks him to make himself comfortable while he goes back to his desk to attend to the next visitor.

This one also wants to see the president.

"The president is in conference just now," the young man replies. "Perhaps there is something I can do for you in the meanwhile if you will tell me what you want."

"It's none of your business," he answers rudely. "I want the president."

The chances are against a man of this sort. He may be a person the president wants to see, but the odds are ten to one that he is not.

"I'm sorry but you cannot possibly see him now. He is busy."

"When will he be free?"

"It is hard to tell. These conferences sometimes last an hour or two, and I am sure he will not see you even then unless you tell him why you want to see him. He is a very busy man."

The visitor sputters around a few minutes and it develops that he is selling insurance. The young man knows that the president will not see him under any circumstances. He is already heavily insured, as every wise man should be, and he cannot be bothered with agents who are trying to sell him larger policies.

"I'm sorry," the young man repeats, "but I am sure there is no use in letting him waste your time. He is already carrying a heavy policy and he positively refuses to talk insurance with anyone, no matter who it is."

This should be enough for the salesman. What the young man says is true. It would be a waste of his time as well as the president's. He does not care half so much for the salesman's time—there is no reason why he should—but notice how tactfully he tells him that the head of the organization has no time to spend with him.

There is a certain rough type of salesman (we use the word salesman here in the broadest sense, as the salesmen themselves use it, to cover all the people who are trying to convince some one else that what they have is worth while whether it is an idea or a washing machine or a packet of drawings)—there is a certain rough type of salesman who tries to bluster his way through. He never lasts long as a salesman, though unfortunately he survives a good many years in various kinds of business. Even he must not be turned away rudely.

"I'm sorry," the young man says to a person of this sort, "but the president has given positive orders that he must not be disturbed this morning. He is engaged in a very important transaction."

The next man who approaches the door has an authentic claim on the president. It would be as great a calamity to turn him away as it would be to let some of the others in. He presents his card and says that he has an appointment. A truly courteous man, whenever possible, arranges an appointment beforehand. The young man takes the card, waves toward the reception room, and asks him to be seated while he finds out if the president is busy. He telephones to the secretary of the president, tells him who is calling, and asks if the president is ready to see him. If the answer is affirmative he asks if he will see him in his office or out in the reception room. It is much easier to get rid of a visitor from the entrance hall or reception room than from an inside office. If he says that he will see him in the reception room the girl reports to the visitor that he will come in a few minutes, offers him a magazine, and asks him to make himself at home. If the president says that he will see the visitor in his office the young man sends one of the messenger boys to usher him through the building.

Now it may be that this man had no appointment with the president, but that he has used it as a pretext to break through. In this case, the secretary answers, after consulting his schedule, that the president has never heard of such a person and has no such appointment. A man of this sort is not worth a minute's consideration. He has shown himself dishonest at the outset with a petty contemptible dishonesty, and the temptation is to pitch him out on his head. But the young man says quietly:

"His secretary says that the president has no appointment with you. I am afraid you have come to the wrong place. It must be some other Mr. Beacon."

There is a note of finality in his voice which convinces the visitor that there is no use in going further.

The next visitor is a woman who has come to have lunch with a friend of hers who works in the accounting department.

"It is fifteen minutes before time for lunch," the young man answers. "I can call her now, of course, but if you would rather not disturb her, I'll tell her that you will wait for her in the reception room until she comes for you."

The woman thanks him and agrees that it will be much better not to disturb her. The young man offers her a chair and a magazine and invites her to make herself comfortable.

It grows monotonous in the telling for him to ask each of the visitors exactly the same questions (never exactly the same, of course) in the same cordial tone of voice and to tell them to make themselves comfortable in exactly the same way, but the means of attaining success in such a place lies in the fact that he greets each visitor as if he were the only one he had to attend to, and that he is, for the time being, at least, completely at the visitor's service. It is not so much what the young man says as the way he says it. "Good morning" can be spoken in such a way that it is an insult.

The Girl at the Telephone. It is nerve-racking to stand at the door to receive callers, but it is much more so to sit at the switchboard and receive messages. The only point of contact is through the voice, but it is remarkable how much of one's personality the voice expresses. If you are tired your voice shows it; if you are cross your voice tells it; if you are worried, your voice betrays it. It is possible for one (everyone) to cultivate a pleasing voice. The telephone companies have learned this, and there is no part of her equipment upon which they spend more time and effort than on the voice of the telephone girl. It is interesting to know that their very excellent motto, "The voice with the smile wins" did not spring into being without thought. On the early bulletins this clumsy phrase was printed: "A smiling voice facilitates service."

The girl at the telephone, even though she receives a thousand calls a day, must answer each one pleasantly and patiently. Some people call without a very clear idea of what they want, and the fact that business houses have so many different names for exactly the same job often makes it difficult for them to locate the person they are asking for, even when they are fairly sure who it is they want.

"May I speak to your personnel manager?" comes the query over the wire to a girl who has never heard of a personnel manager.

"I'm sorry, I did not quite hear you."

The person at the other end repeats the word and the girl is sure she had it right the first time.

"We have no personnel manager here. Maybe there is some one else who would do. If you will tell me what you want——"

"I want a job."

"Just a minute, please, I'll connect you with our employment manager."

Advertising engineers, executive secretaries,

and many others are old jobs masquerading under new names.

More business men complain of the girl at the telephone than of any other person in business. She must, under the handicap of distance, accomplish exactly what the man at the door does, and must do it as efficiently and as courteously.

No matter how angry the one who is calling becomes, no matter how profane he may be, no matter what he says, she must not answer back, and she must not slam the receiver down while he is talking. Perfect poise, an even temper, patience, and a pleasant voice under control—if she has these, and a vast number of the telephone girls have, she need not worry about the rules of courtesy. They will take care of themselves.

The numbers that a girl in a business office has to call frequently she should have on a pad or card near the switchboard so that she will not have to look them up. Many business men ask the girl at the board to give them Blank and Blank or Smith and Smith instead of giving her the numbers of the two concerns. She then has to look them up, quite a difficult task when one has the headpiece on and calls coming in and going out every minute. To stop to look up one number often delays several, and it is a duty which should never devolve upon the girl whose business it is to send the calls through. The man who is calling, or his secretary, if he has one, or a person near the switchboard stationed there for the purpose should look up the numbers and give them to the operator.

An efficient girl at the telephone sends numbers through as quickly as is humanly possible, but even then she is often scolded by nervous and harassed men who expect more than can really be done.

Mr. Hunter has called Main 6785. It is busy. He waits. Hours pass. At least it seems so to him, and he grows impatient.

"What's the matter with that number, Miss Fisher?"

"I'm still trying, Mr. Hunter. I'll call you when they answer."

The line continues busy. Mr. Hunter looks over the papers on his desk. His nervousness increases. He takes down the receiver again and asks what the trouble is. He does not get the number any more quickly this way, but it would be hard to convince him that he does not. The girl says quietly again that she is still trying. He clings to the receiver and in a few minutes she answers triumphantly, "Here they are," and the connection is made.

The telephone girl in a big concern (or a little one) is constantly annoyed with people who have the wrong number. When it happens ten or twelve times in the course of a day—fortunately it is not usually so often—it is hard for her to keep a grip on her temper and answer pleasantly, "This is not the number you want," but the snappish answer always makes a bad situation worse, and the loss of temper which causes it drains the energy of the person who makes it. It is not merely the voice with the smile that wins; it is the disposition and temperament to which such a voice is the index.

The Secretary. The next in the line of defense is the president's secretary. To him (and we use the masculine pronoun although this position, like a good many others, is often held by women even in the biggest organizations, where the responsibility attached to it is by no means small)—to him the president turns over the details of his day's work. He arranges the president's schedule and reminds him of the things he has forgotten and the things he is likely to forget. He receives all of his visitors by telephone first and many times disposes of their wants without having to connect them with the president at all. He receives many of the callers who are admitted by the man at the door and in the same way often takes care of them without disturbing the president. He knows more about the petty routine of the job than the president himself. He is accurate. He is responsible. He is patient. He is courteous.

In order that he may be all these things it is necessary for the president to keep him well informed as to what he is doing and where he is going and what he is planning so that he can give intelligent answers to the people who come, so that he can keep things running smoothly when the president is away, so that he can answer without delay when the president asks whether he has a luncheon engagement on Thursday, and what he did with the memorandum from the circulation manager, and who is handling the shipping sheets.

Men who have their minds on larger matters cannot keep all the details of their jobs in mind, but it is significant to know that most successful business men know with more than a fair degree of accuracy what these details amount to. Some secretaries feel very superior to the men who employ them because they can remember the date on which the representatives of the Gettem Company called and the employers cannot. The author knows a chauffeur who drives for a famous New York surgeon who thinks himself a much better man than the surgeon because he can remember the numbers of the houses where his patients and his friends live and the surgeon cannot. The author also knows a messenger boy who thinks himself a much bigger man than one of the most successful brokers in Wall Street because the broker sometimes gives him the same message twice within fifteen minutes, the second time after it has already been delivered.

The secretary comes to the office every morning neatly clad and on time. The hour at which his employer comes in has nothing to do with him. There is a definite time at which he is expected to be at his desk. He is there.

He opens the letters on his desk—and those addressed to the president come first to him—and sorts them, throwing aside the worthless advertising matter, saving that which may be of some interest, marking the letters that are to be referred to various other members of the house, and placing them in the memorandum basket, piling into one heap those that he cannot answer without first consulting the president, and into another those which must be answered by the president personally. Intimately personal letters often come mixed in with the rest of the mail. No man wants a secretary whom he cannot trust even with letters of this sort, but almost any secretary worth having will feel a certain amount of delicacy in opening them unless he is requested to do so. When these letters are from people who write often the secretary grows to recognize the handwriting from the outside of the envelope, and therefore does not need to open them. In other cases it is sometimes possible to distinguish a personal from a business letter. These should be handled according to the wishes of the man to whom they are directed. Many business men turn practically everything—even the settlement of their family affairs—over to their secretaries. It is a personal matter, and the secretary's part in it is to carry out the wishes of his employer.

By the time the mail is sorted the president has come in.

He rings for his secretary, telephones for him, sends a messenger for him, or else goes to his desk himself and asks him to come in and take dictation. There is no special courtesy or discourtesy in any of these methods. It depends on how far apart the desks are, how busy he is, and a number of other things. He does not yell for his secretary to come in. He manages to get him there quietly. It is not necessary for him to rise when the secretary enters (even if the secretary is a woman) though he may do so (and it is a very gracious thing, especially if the secretary is a woman) but he should greet him (or her) with a pleasant "Good-morning."

The secretary takes his place in the comfortable chair that has been provided for him, with notebook and pencil in hand and at least one pencil in reserve. He waits for the president to begin, and listens closely so that he may transcribe as rapidly as he speaks. If he fails to understand he waits until they come to the end of a sentence before asking his employer to repeat. It is much better to do so then than to depend on puzzling it out later or coming back and asking him after he has forgotten what was said.

Telephone interruptions and others may come during the dictation but the secretary waits until he is dismissed or until the pile of letters has disappeared.

When the president has finished it is the secretary's time to begin talking. He consults him about the various letters upon which he needs his advice and makes notations in shorthand on them. He reports on the various calls that have come in and the house memoranda. A good secretary reads and digests these before turning them over to his employer, and in most cases gives the gist of the memorandum instead of the memorandum itself. It saves time.

The president's secretary usually has a secretary of his own, a woman, let us say, or a girl whose preliminary training has been good and whose record for the year and a half she has been with the company has been excellent.

She comes to her desk on time every morning as fresh as a daisy and as inconspicuous. The relation that she bears to the president's secretary is much the same as the relation that he bears to the president. She gets the letters that are addressed to him and sorts them in the same way that he does those of the president. On days when he is absent she takes care of all of his work, in so far as she is able, as well as her own.

Her employer is considerate of her always. He does not make a practice of taking ten or fifteen minutes of her lunch hour or five or ten minutes overtime at the close of the day, but when there is a good reason why he should ask her to remain he does so, asking courteously if she would mind staying. If she is genuinely interested in her work—and this young lady is— she will stay, but if she has an even better reason why she should go she explains briefly that it is impossible to stay. He never imposes heavier burdens upon her than she can bear, but he does not hesitate to ask her to do whatever needs to be done, and he does it with a "Please" and a "Thank you," and not with a "See, here" and a "Say, listen to me, now." She is a very pretty and attractive girl, but the man she is working for is a gentleman. To him she is his secretary, and if he were ever in danger of forgetting it she would be quick to remind him. She does not go around with a chip on her shoulder all the time, and she talks freely with the various men around the office just as she does with the women and girls, but it is in an impersonal way. She never permits intimate attentions from her immediate employer or any one else.

Executives. "Executive" is a large, loose word which rolls smoothly off the tongue of far too many business men to-day. Office boys begin to think in terms of it before they are out of knee trousers. "I could hold down the job," said a youngster who had hurt his hand and whose business was to carry a bag of mail from a suburban factory into New York, "if I could get some one to carry the bag." "I can do the work," say smart young men in the "infant twenties" (and many others—there is no age limit), "but I must have a man to look after the details."

The way to an executive position is through details. Work, plain hard work, is the foundation of every enduring job, and the executive who thinks he can do without it has a sharp reckoning day ahead. In most places the executives have worked their way up slowly, and at no time along the way have they had that large contempt for small jobs which characterizes so many young men in business. They have been perfectly willing to do whatever came to hand.

But after all this is said, the fact remains that an executive is successful not so much because of his own ability as because of his power to recognize ability in other men. He is—and this is true of every executive from the president down —the servant of his people in much the same way that the President of the United States is the servant of the American people. This means that he must be readily accessible to them, and must listen as courteously to them as if they were important visitors from across the sea or somewhere else.

Many executives—and this was true especially during the war—have surrounded themselves with a tangle of red tape which has to be unwound every time an employee (or any one else) wants to get near enough to ask a question. This is absurd. Sensible men destroy elaborate plans of management and find they get along better without them. The Baldwin Locomotive Works,

which has a hundred years of solid reputation behind it, has no management plans. "There is
about the place an atmosphere of work, and work
without frills or feathers," and this is essentially
true of every business that is built to last. Look
at the organizations which, because of war conditions, rose into a prosperity they had never enjoyed before. Most of them have collapsed, and
the little men who rose with them (so many of
them and so much too small for their jobs) have
collapsed with them.

In the big reliable concerns, and the small
ones, too, the high executives are easily approached, especially by the members of the
organization. In many of the open offices—and
open offices have done much to create a feeling
of comradeship among workers—the desk of the
general manager is out on the floor with the
desks of the rank and file of the employees with
nothing to distinguish it from theirs except the
fact that there is a bigger man behind it. A real
man does not need a lot of elaborate decorations.
They annoy him.

There are two sides to this, however. Visitors
from the outside are not the only ones who are
likely to waste the time of other people, and a
busy man has to protect himself from indoor
nuisances as well as those that drift in from the

outside. Some do it by means of secretaries, but a good executive needs no barrier at all between himself and his own men. They learn soon enough—we are speaking now of a good executive, remember—that there is no use in going to him unless there is some definite reason why they should, and that the more briefly and directly they present their problem the more likely they are to have it settled.

When an executive receives a caller (or when any man in a business house receives a caller) he should *receive* him and not merely tolerate him. A young advertising man who began several years ago had two very interesting experiences with two gruff executives in two different companies. Both consented to see him, both kept on writing at their desks after he entered and gave him scant attention throughout the interview. Apparently they were both successful business men. Certainly they both held positions that would indicate it. Yet both of them a few years later came to the young advertising man at different times looking for jobs. Needless to say neither found a place with him, not because he held a grudge against them, but simply because he knew what kind of men they were and that they could not help in the kind of business he was trying to build.

From the beginning of the interview the host should do all he can to make his visitor comfortable. You see a lot in certain magazines about setting the visitor at a disadvantage by giving him an awkward chair, making him face the light and grilling him with questions. It is pure nonsense.

It is very gracious for a man to rise to greet a caller and extend his hand, especially if the caller is young and ill at ease. It is imperative if it is an old man or a woman. He should ask the visitor to be seated before he sits down himself.

"Well, young man, what can I do for you?" is hardly a polite way of opening an interview. The host should wait with a cordially receptive air until his guest begins, unless he is in a great hurry. Then he frankly tells the caller so and asks him to make his business brief.

Interruptions come even in the midst of conversations with important visitors, but no visitor is so important as to permit neglect of one's employees. These should be met courteously and dispatched quickly. The host must always ask the pardon of the guest before turning to the telephone or to a messenger, and if the guest is an employee the rule is the same.

At the conclusion of the interview the host

rises and shakes hands with the departing visitor but does not necessarily go with him (or her) to the door or the elevator, as the case may be. This is an additional courtesy in which a busy man cannot always indulge. The essential part of every interview is that the visitor shall state what he wants, that the host shall give the best answer in his power, and then the sooner the visitor departs the better for all concerned.

The Rank and File. This is the largest group in every business. It is the one that fluctuates most. It is the one from which the discards are made. It is the one from which officers are chosen. It is the one in which the real growth of a business takes place. And by the same token it is the one, generally speaking, where there is most discourtesy. Promotion depends upon the possession of this quality much more than people realize. Many a man with actual ability to hold a high position is not given an opportunity to do so because the men who employ him realize that he would antagonize those who worked under him.

There are among the body of employees in every concern (even the very best) discontented members. In most cases, indeed, in nearly all cases except where there is a chronic grudge against life which is not affected by external circumstances, these are weeded out, and those with habitual grudges are weeded out along with the others or else are kept in minor places. Perhaps it would be more nearly correct to say they keep themselves there. Sometimes a subordinate feels that he is unfairly treated by his immediate superior. He wishes to go to the man above him in authority. Is it right for him to do so?

It is an unwritten law that each worker shall be loyal to the head of his department. Suppose the head does not deserve it?

There are three courses open to the worker. He can leave the job and find another in a different organization. He can go to the head of the department and state the case to him. If this should fail he may appeal to the man above him, but *he should never go over the head of his own immediate superior without first telling him that he intends to do it.*

This is an important rule. It holds whether one has a grievance to present or a suggestion. Constructive plans should first be talked over with one's immediate superior, and with his approval carried to the next man, or he may carry them himself. If this superior is the sort of man with whom you are constantly at loggerheads, you had much better get out and get a place somewhere else. And if you find that continu-

ally you are in hot water with the men who have
authority over you, you may be very sure that
the fault is not altogether theirs.

Subordinates usually have an idea that the
heads of their departments leave all of the work
to them. Well, as a matter of fact, they do leave
a large part of it. If they did not they would
have no excuse for having subordinates. The
reward of good work is more work. This is less
of a hardship than it sounds. Sir James Barrie
once quoted Dr. Johnson's statement that doubtless the Lord could have made a better fruit than
the strawberry, but that he doubtless never did,
and added to it that He doubtless could have
created something that was more fun than hard
work, but that He doubtless never did.

The subway guards in New York City say
that the rush which comes just before five o'clock
(the closing time of most of the business houses)
is as great as the one which comes just after.
They call the persons in the former rush the
clock watchers. They have left work about fifteen minutes early, and to-morrow morning—
business experience has taught this—they will
come in fifteen minutes late. For the most part
these are the discontented workers who spend
"60 per cent. of their time in doing their job, and
40 per cent. in doing the boss."

It has always been considered a breach of good manners to pull out one's watch and look at it in company. It is true in the office as well as in the drawing room. The clock watchers are impolite. It has also been considered a breach of good manners to hold a guest against his will against the conventional hour for his departure. The employers who habitually keep their employees after closing hours are equally impolite. It is a question of honor, too. Time is money, and the time grafters, whether employers or employees, are dishonest.

When one employee goes over to the desk of another it is not necessary for the second to rise. The first should wait until the one at the desk looks up before speaking unless he is so absorbed in his work that he does not glance up after a minute or two. Then he should interrupt with "I beg your pardon." It makes no difference if one of the employees is a woman and the other is a man. Work at an office can be seriously impeded if every time one person goes to the desk of another the other rises. So many times the whole conversation covers less time than it takes to get out of one's chair and sit back down again. In some places subordinates are required to stand when a superior speaks to them, but as a general thing it is not necessary. In such houses it is correct to play the game according to the general standard and to act according to the rules set down by the men who are in charge of affairs.

There is no person so wretched or so poor or so miserable but that he can find other people who are more wretched, poorer, or more miserable. At the same time there is no person so superior, so wealthy, or gifted but that he can find other people who are more superior, more wealthy, and more gifted. It is a part of good manners to recognize superiority when one finds it. Youngsters entering business can sit at the feet of the older men in the same business and learn a great deal. Knowledge did not enter the world with the present generation any more than it will depart from it when the present generation dies. It is just as well for young people to realize this. Age has much to teach them. Experience has much to teach them, and so have men and women of extraordinary ability. "I have never met a man," says a teacher of business men, "from whom I could not learn something." All of us are born with the capacity to learn. It is those who develop it who amount to something.

Petty quarrels should be disregarded and grudges should be forgotten. This piece of ad-

vice is needed more by women in business than
by men. Men have learned—it has taken them
several thousand years—to fight and shake
hands. They have a happy way of forgetting
their squabbles—this is a general truth—after
a little while, and two men who were yesterday
abusing one another with hot and angry words
are to-day walking together down the hall smiling and talking as gently as you please.

The Office Boy. If the office boy in a big
business house where much of the work is done
at a white-hot tension—the office boy in a busy
Wall Street office during the peak of the day's
rush, for example—could write his intimate impressions they would make good reading.

The temper of the great American business
man is an uncertain quantity. Famous for good
humor and generosity as a general thing, he is,
for all that, at his worst moments the terror of
the office boy's life. Nervous, worried, tired,
and exasperated, he is likely to "take it out" on
the office boy if there is no one else at hand.
There is no defense for such conduct—even the
man who is guilty would not, the next day in his
calmer moments, defend it. Meantime, what
shall the office boy do?

A hot, tired man with papers fluttering over
his desk, his telephone ringing, and three men

waiting in line to talk to him about serious problems connected with the business, yells, "What
do you want?" when the office boy comes to
answer the bell.

"You rang for me," the boy answers.

"I rang half an hour ago," the man snaps.

In reality he rang two minutes before. Shall
the office boy remind him of this?

Not if he values his job!

Of course it is unjust, but one of the first laws
of discipline is to learn to be composed in the
face of injustice, and the first law of courtesy
for the office boy (and other employees would do
just as well to follow) is: Don't be too harsh with
the boss!

It is said that the grizzly bear, who is a very
strict mother, often spanks her cubs when she
herself has done something foolish. Julia Ellen
Rogers tells a story of an explorer who came
suddenly upon a bear with two cubs. He was so
frightened that he stood still for a minute or two
before he could decide which way to run. Meantime the bear, fully as frightened as he, turned
and fled, spanking the two cubs at every jump
in spite of the fact that each was already going
as fast as its legs could carry it. "It was so un-
expected," continues Miss Rogers, "and so funny
to see those little bears look around reproach-

fully at their angry parent every time they felt the weight of her paw, helping them to hurry, that the man sat down and laughed until he cried."

It was not funny to the cubs.

Cases in which the office boy is maltreated are exceptional, though cases in which he is misunderstood are not. Most office boys have not one boss but many. There should always be one person from whom they receive their general orders and to whom they go with their troubles. (A youngster should have very few troubles to report. It is usually the worthless ones who report.)

In most places the several office boys are stationed at a certain point, a desk or a table, with one of their number more or less in charge. The rule is that one person be always at the desk.

All right. Six office boys. Five out on errands. One at the desk. The bell rings. The boy keeps his place. The bell rings again. The boy keeps his place. The bell rings a third time, long and insistently, but the youngster, with a steadfastness worthy of the boy who stood on the burning deck, still keeps his place.

A second later an angry official bounces out and wants to know what on earth is the matter

and declares that he will report the desk to the
manager.   Meanwhile one of the missing five
has returned, and the youngster who had held
the place so long under fire takes the message
from the man and delivers it.

If the boy should see an opening—and most
business men except those funny little executives
puffed up with their own importance are ready
enough to listen—he may explain how it happened, but if he has to enter a shouting contest
it is best to stay silent.

The law of business courtesy—no matter how
far away from this a discussion goes it always
swings back—is the Golden Rule.   The subordinate who feels himself neglected by the men in
positions above him might check himself by honestly asking himself how he appears to those
beneath him.   It is interesting to know that the
one who complains most is usually the one who is
haughtiest when he enters into conversation with
the employees, who, he thinks, are not quite worth
his notice.   He feels blighted because the president does not stop to say "Good-morning" in
the hall, but it is beneath his dignity to say
"Good-morning" to the girl who collects his mail
or "Good-night" to the janitor who comes to
dust his desk when the day's work is over.   The
means of attaining courtesy—and if you have

it yourself you will find it in other people—
is by watching your own actions. Teach no
one but yourself. Worry about no one's behavior but your own. That is job enough for
any one.

XI

IN A DEPARTMENT STORE

LET us now see courtesy at work in a big department store.

Mr. Hopkins has taken a morning off to do a little shopping before he goes away on his summer vacation. He wants to buy two shirts, a trunk, a toy for his baby, and a present for his wife. He is not sure what he wants for the wife and baby.

Mr. Hopkins does not like to shop. He remembers his last expedition. A haberdashery had sent him a cordial letter asking him to open an account. He did so, but one morning later when he went in to buy a waistcoat the rude and inefficient service he met disgusted him so that he has not been back since. He knew exactly what he wanted and asked for it. "Oh, no," answered the smart young clerk. "You don't want that. People have not been wearing waistcoats like that for years. This is what you want," and he exhibited a different style altogether. It happened that Mr. Hopkins knew better than the clerk what he wanted, and the fact that people had not been wearing waistcoats like it made no difference to him.   As a matter of fact, the only reason the clerk made the remark was that he did not have them in stock, and thought perhaps he could sell by substituting.

There are other haberdasheries where the service is distinctly good, but Mr. Hopkins decides to go to a department store instead.   Haberdasheries, however excellent, do not carry toys for one's baby nor presents for one's wife.

Helpem's store has been warmly recommended.   He will go there.   It is his first visit.

When he enters the door he is bewildered by an array of women's scarfs and gloves and perfume bottles, handkerchiefs and parasols, handbags, petticoats, knick-knacks, and whatnot.   He almost loses courage and begins backing toward the door when he catches sight of a man in uniform standing near the entrance.   He sees that this man is directing the tides of shoppers that are surging in, and approaches him.

"Where can I find the trunks?"

"Third floor.   Elevator in the rear," the man answers briefly (but not gruffly).   People who have to answer thousands of questions must be brief.

As he passes down the aisle Mr. Hopkins, who

is very observant, notices that all of the girls—
most of the clerks are girls—are dressed in a
pleasant gray. This gives an agreeable uniform
tone to a large establishment which would break
up into jarring patches of color if each clerk
were allowed to wear whatever color happened to
strike her fancy. Good idea, Mr. Hopkins
thinks, very necessary where there are many,
many clerks.

He does not have much trouble getting the
trunk. He knows pretty well what he wants,
and the obliging salesman convinces him that
the trunk will probably last forever by assuring
him that an elephant could dance a jig on it and
never make a dent. He asks Mr. Hopkins if he
wants his name on it. Mr. Hopkins had not
thought of it, but he does. No, upon second
thought, he will have only his initials stenciled
on in dull red, W. H. H. The trunk will be
delivered in the afternoon and he goes away well
satisfied.

The shirts are somewhat more difficult. He is
attached to a certain kind of collar and he likes
madras shirts with little black stripes or figures
in them. The man shows him white ones and
wide striped ones and colored ones with the right
collar, and he almost decides that the place does
not keep madras shirts with little black figures

in them, when he suddenly realizes that he was so intent on getting the collar that he forgot to say anything about the material or color. He begins again, tells the clerk exactly what he wants, and in a few minutes the proper shirts are before him and he is happy. While the clerk is folding them, he asks about ties. It is a good thing. Mr. Hopkins remembers that he has forgotten ties. They have great bargains in ties. He drifts over to the counter and presently has three lovely ones. One is red, and Mr. Hopkins resolves to be more careful than he was with the last red one. His wife burned it. He must keep this hidden.

The ties remind him that he needs a bathrobe. An agreeable clerk sells him a dull figured bath-robe, comfortable and light for summer and guaranteed to wash, and tells him that a pajama sale is in progress about four counters away.

When he has bought six pairs of pajamas he begins to think of the baby's present. Toys are on the top floor. The girl there—a wise department store always chooses carefully for this place—is very helpful. She asks about the baby, how old he is, what toys he has, what toys he has asked for, and so on. Mr. Hopkins tells her, and after showing him several ingenious mechanical contrivances, she suggests a train with a real track to run on. Mr. Hopkins is delighted.

The girl asks if the youngster likes to read. He does not, but he likes to be read to. "Why don't you take him a book?" and in a few minutes he has the "Just-So Stories" tucked under his arm. As he leaves the girl smiles, "Come back to see us," she says.

All the clerks have said this. The clerk who sold the shirts said, while they stood waiting for the change, that he could depend on them. They would not shrink and the colors would not run. "We are here in the city," he continued (the store was in New York), "but we have our regular customers just as if we were in a small town. We don't try to make just one sale and get by with it. We want you to come back."

The girl at the toy counter tells Mr. Hopkins that there is a woman downstairs who will help him select something for his wife. He goes back to the man in uniform to locate her and finds her in a secluded booth on the first floor. She asks several questions about whether he would like china or silver, furniture or linen, but Mr. Hopkins wants to give his wife something personal—something she can use or wear. He has been married several years but not long enough to know that this is a dangerous thing to do, but the woman is wise. She suggests a silk parasol, a kimono, or a dozen handkerchiefs.

Such a service as this is not possible except in very large shops, but in most places clerks are quick to respond with suggestions for gifts. There is a pleasure about buying them and selling them that does not go with ordinary transactions.

When he buys a parasol the clerk suggests that they have a very large assortment of handbags, but Mr. Hopkins's day's work is done, and the clerk does not insist. None of the clerks in a good department store is insistent. They offer suggestions and stand ready to serve, but they do not try to impose their ideas or their goods upon the customers. Mr. Hopkins leaves well satisfied with himself and his purchases. He will come back.

The trunk is delivered in the afternoon, not by the regular wagon, but by an express company. It is a busy season. Mr. Hopkins is still further delighted. These people keep their promises. And as he tips the man who brought it up —he had to climb three flights of stairs—the man gives him a card. "Here's one of the boss's cards," he says, "in case you want any hauling done." Without doubt the man has been instructed by the boss to distribute his cards, but he does it with such a grace that it seems to be on his own initiative.

It rarely happens that a business man or woman can shop in the leisurely manner described above. Most of their shopping has to be done during the half hour after lunch or during a frantic few minutes snatched at the beginning or the end of the day's work. One morning Mr. Hopkins had to leave home without a collar because he forgot to send the dirty ones to the laundry (his wife was away that week) and dashed into a little shop to get one on the way to the office. He would have felt like murdering a clerk who wanted to show him something nice in the way of gloves or mufflers, and he would have had a hard time to restrain himself from violence if the clerk had started in on a eulogy of a new shipment of English tweeds.

An intelligent clerk can usually tell when his customer is in a tearing hurry. It is an unpropitious time to make suggestions. The clerk must see things from the customer's point of view. It is permissible to suggest something else in place of the thing he has asked for but it is not good manners to make fun of it or to insist upon a substitute. Recently a woman wanted to buy a rug for her automobile. She knew just what she wanted, but the bright young clerk insisted that she wanted something else. She finally bought the rug, but it was in spite of the clerk rather than because of him. Too many salesmen kill their sales by thinking and talking only of their product. The customer is not half so interested in that as he is in himself. Good salesmanship relates the product to the customer, and does it in such a way that the customer is hardly aware of how it is done.

XII

A WHILE WITH A TRAVELING MAN

In a Big City. We will suppose that our traveling man has his headquarters in some big city—New York, Chicago, San Francisco, it does not matter—and that he has several calls to make before he goes out on the road.

There are two kinds of salesmen, those who make only one sale to a customer and those who sell something that has to be renewed periodically. The first sell pianos, real estate, encyclopedias, and so on; the second sell raw materials and supplies. The salesman whom we are to follow is in the second group.

He has—and so have most men who do this kind of selling—a regular routine that he follows, adding new names to the list and deleting old ones as seems expedient. At this particular time he has several old customers to visit and one or two new prospects to investigate before he leaves town.

It is unnecessary for him to make arrange-

ments beforehand to gain access to the old customers. They know him and they are always
glad to see him. But if there is a chance that the
customer may be out of town, or if it is during a
busy season, he telephones ahead to make sure.
He prefers indefinite to definite appointments,
especially if he has to see two or three people during the course of a morning or an afternoon; that
is, he would rather have an appointment to come
some time between ten and eleven or between
three and four than to have one for exactly half
past ten or a quarter of three. It is impossible
to tell how long interviews will last. Sometimes
when the salesman counts on staying an hour he
is through in five minutes and sometimes when
he thinks he can arrange things in fifteen minutes
he finds himself strung up for half a day.

The new prospects—there are three on this
particular morning—he handles in different
ways. To one he has a note of introduction from
a mutual friend. To another he has written a
letter stating why he wishes to call and asking
when it will be convenient for him to do so. The
third, whom he knows by reputation as a "hard
customer" (in the slang sense of the word) who
will have nothing to do with salesmen of any sort,
he decides to approach directly, trusting to his
own presence to get past the girl at the front door

and whomsoever else stands between him and the man he wants to see. He does not write, because he knows that the man would tear up the letter and he does not telephone, because he knows that the man would not promise to see him and that if he were to call after such a telephone conversation his chances for success would be lessened.

Our salesman is careful with his appearance. He bathes and shaves every morning and takes special care that his linen is clean and that his shoes are polished. He does not ornament himself with a lot of jewelry, and the material of which his suit is made is plain. He presents, if you should see him on the street, the appearance of a clean, solid, healthy, progressive American citizen. He is poised but he is not aggressive. He is persistent but he is not obstinate.

The best public speakers, it is said, never get over a sinking feeling of fear during the few minutes just before time for them to speak. It vanishes as soon as they get to their feet or a very few minutes afterward, and, strange as it may seem, it is this very fear that gives them their power on the platform. The fact that they have the dreadful feeling nerves them to strenuous effort, and it is this effort that makes the orator. In the same way the best salesmen are those who never get over the fear that perhaps they have not thought out the best way to handle the situation ahead of them. They forget the fear as they begin to talk to the prospect, but the fact that it is subconsciously present makes the difference between the real salesman and the "dub."

Did you ever get to the door of a house you were about to enter and then turn and walk around the block before you rang the bell? Did you ever walk around the block six or eight times? So have we. Especially on those Wednesday and Sunday evenings when we used to go calling. There are not many salesmen who have not had this experience and who have not, upon hearing that a prospect they dreaded was out, turned away from the door with a prayer of deep thanksgiving. All of which is by way of saying that selling is not an easy job.

The salesman whose career we are following for a short time always has that little feeling of nervousness before an interview. It is deeper than ever when he approaches the "hard customer," and it is not lessened in the least degree when he finds a painted and marceled flapper at the door who looks at him without a word. (Incidentally, she likes his looks.)

He takes out his card and asks her to give it to Mr. Green and say that he is calling.

"He won't see you," the girl says.

"Will you tell him, please, that I am here, all the same? Wait a minute."

He takes the card and scribbles on it, "I want only five minutes of your time," and hands it to the girl again.

She carries it away and presently returns saying that Mr. Green is busy and cannot see him.

"I knew he wouldn't," she adds.

"He must be very busy," the salesman says. "When shall I be most likely to find him free?"

"He's no busier now than usual," the girl responds. "He's smoking a cigar and looking out the window."

"Will you tell him, please, that I am coming back to-morrow at the same time?"

The girl sees that he is very much in earnest. She respects him for his quiet persistence and because he has not tried to "kid" her. She would most likely have joined in heartily if he had, but he would never have got past her.

She goes back into the office and returns with word that the salesman may come in if he will not take more than five minutes. He thanks the girl and goes into the office where the "hard customer" is seated. He does not rise, he does not say "Good morning," and he does not take the

cigar out of his mouth, but this does not discon-
cert the salesman.   He wastes no time in pre-
liminaries, but after a brief greeting, plunges at
once into his proposition, stating the essential
points clearly and in terms of this man's business.   He knows what the customer needs pretty
accurately for he has taken the trouble to find
out.   He is not broadcasting.   He is using line
radio, and everything he says is directed against
a single mark.   The prospect is interested.   He
puts the cigar aside.   The salesman concludes.

"I'm sorry," he says, "but my five minutes are
up.   Will you let me come back some day when
you are not so busy and tell you more about it?"

"Sit where you are," the other says, and begins
firing questions.

Half an hour later the salesman pockets the
order he wanted and makes ready to depart, feeling that he has found another friend.   The "hard
customer" is ashamed of his gruff reception and
apologizes for it.   "I've been so bothered with
agents and drummers and traveling men that
I've promised myself never to see another one as
long as I live," he says.

"I can well understand that," the salesman answers.   "It is one of the hardest things we are
up against, the fact that there are so many four-
flushers out trying to sell things."

He goes next to see the man with whom he has made an appointment by mail and finds that he has been called out of town on business. He talks with his secretary, who expresses a polite regret that they were unable to locate him in time to tell him that his visit would be of no use. He asks if there is some one else who can take charge of the matter, but the girl replies that all such things have to come before Mr. Thompson. He will not be back until next week, and by that time the salesman will be out on the road.

"I'll have another representative of our house, Mr. Hamilton, call," he says. "He will write to find out when it will be convenient for him to come."

The third man on his list is the one to whom he has the letter of introduction. This is one of his best prospects. That is why he took such pains to arm himself with the letter. He has no trouble getting inside. The man is very busy but he thrusts it completely aside for the moment. He does not have to say "Be brief." Our salesman has been in the game long enough to know that he must not be anything else.

"Frankly," he says at the end of the talk, "I am not interested. I have no doubt that what you say is true. In fact, I have heard of your firm before and know that its reputation is good.

But I buy my material, and have for years, from Hicks and Hicks."

"It is a good reliable concern," the salesman responds, "and there is no reason why you should desert them. They depend upon you as much as you do upon them. But if they happen to be short of something you want in a hurry, please remember that our product is as good as theirs. You can depend upon it with as much certainty."

"Thank you, I will," the prospect answers and the interview is over.

Did the salesman act wisely? Would he have gained anything by proving that his house was superior to Hicks and Hicks? Not if the customer was worth having. This salesman never forgets that his part of the job is to build up business for his own firm, and not to tear down business for other firms. As it stands, he has in this case established a feeling of good will for the house he represents, and has placed it in such a light that if the rival concern should be afflicted with a strike or a fire or any of a hundred or two disasters which might lessen or suspend its output, the customer will probably turn to the salesman's house. And if Hicks and Hicks should sell out or go into bankruptcy the salesman will have won for his own house a steady customer of great value.

In the Sleeping Car. The wise traveling man —and our salesman is wise—always engages sleeping accommodations on the train in advance. This time he has the lower berth in No. 9.

When he comes in to take his seat he finds that a woman has the upper berth in the same compartment. He is reading a newspaper and she is reading a magazine. He says nothing until toward evening, and then he offers to exchange places with her. She thanks him cordially, explains that she was late in securing a berth and that this was all she could get. She is very grateful and the transfer is made.

He goes into the smoking car and meets there several men who are talking together. He joins them and the conversation runs along pleasantly enough until one of the number begins to retail dirty stories. Some of the others try to switch him off to another subject but he is wound up and nothing short of a sledge hammer will stop him until he has run down. Our salesman has a healthy loathing for this sort of thing. He has a good fund of stories himself—most traveling men have—and in the course of his journeyings he has heard many of the kind that the foul-minded man in the smoking car is retailing with such delight. He never retells stories of that nature, and he never, when he can avoid it, listens to them. He knows that he cannot stop the man, but after a little while he gets up quietly and leaves. Another man follows him and the two stand on the rear platform of the train until time to go to bed.

Men who are traveling together often converse without knowing one another's names, and it is correct that they should. Only a prig refuses to speak to a man on a train or a boat because he does not know his name. Opening conversation with a stranger is not always easy, and should be avoided unless it comes about in a natural way. The stranger may not want to converse. It is correct for a man who wishes to talk to another first to introduce himself. "My name is Hammond," he says, and the man to whom he says it responds by holding out his hand (this is the more gracious way, but he may omit this part of it, if he likes) and pronouncing his own name. The same rule holds when the travelers are women.

Our salesman goes to bed early.

Two men have the compartment across from his. They seem very much interested in each other, for they continue to talk after they have gone to bed. In order to make themselves heard they have almost to scream, and the raucous sound of their voices is much more disturbing than the sound of the wheels grinding against the rails. It is hard to sleep on a train even under favorable circumstances. Our salesman has a strenuous day ahead of him—most of his days are strenuous—and the noise is keeping him awake.

He could throw on his bathrobe, climb down and remonstrate with the two men across the way. It would be correct for him to do so, but it would hardly be expedient. People who are thoughtless enough to be noisy late at night are often rude enough to be very unpleasant when any one interferes. The salesman has no real authority over them, but the porter on duty at night is supposed to see that a certain amount of peace and quiet is maintained. The sales-man rings the bell, and when the porter appears, asks him if he would mind begging the two men across the aisle to lower their voices. The porter has had years of experience. He has developed a soft, pleasant way of asking people to be quiet, and in a few minutes the car is still except for the inevitable sound of the train and the snor-ing of an old lady near the end of the car. This last cannot be helped. It must be endured, and our salesman composes himself into a deep slumber.

Dressing and undressing in a sleeping car are among the most difficult operations to perform gracefully.   There are no rules.   Most men prefer staying in their berths to making the attempt in the crowded dressing rooms.   Some divide the process between the two, but no gentleman ever goes streaking down the aisle half-dressed. He is either fully clothed or else he is wrapped in a bathrobe or a dressing gown.

When our salesman comes in to breakfast the next morning there is only one vacant place, a seat opposite a young woman at a table for two.   He crosses over and sits down, first asking if he may do so.   In well-managed dining cars and restaurants, the seating is taken care of by the head waiter.   He never places a person at a table with some one else without asking permission of the one who is already seated.   It is never permissible for a stranger to go to a table that is already taken if there is a vacant one available.   The young lady bows and smiles. She has already sent in her order.   They talk during the meal quite as if they had been introduced and had met by appointment instead of by accident.   She does not introduce herself, nor does he introduce himself.   When she has finished she asks the waiter for her bill.   She pays it herself—our salesman has too much delicacy to offer to do so—and tips the water. Then with a nod and a smile she is gone.

This salesman is a chivalrous traveler. Whenever there is an opportunity to render a service to a woman (or to any one else) he takes pleasure in doing it. He does not place women under financial obligation to him, however, and he is careful not to annoy them with attentions. He has many times found a taxi for a woman traveling alone or with children when they have had the same destination; he has helped women decipher time tables; he has carried bundles and suitcases and baskets and boxes for old ladies who have not yet learned in all their long, long lives that the way to travel is with as little, instead of with as much, baggage as possible; and he has helped young mothers establish themselves comfortably in place with their children. But he has never—and he has been traveling a good many years now—thrust himself upon a woman and he has never embarrassed one by his attentions.

He does not "treat" the men whom he meets by accident during his travels. They often go in to meals together but each one settles his own bill, and when they come to the end of the journey they are without obligations toward one another. It is much pleasanter so.

The salesman does not, as a rule, tip the porter until he leaves the train, and the amount that he gives then is according to what the porter has done for him. If he has been in the car a good many hours and if he has had to ask the porter for many things, such as bringing ice water at night, silencing objectionable travelers, bringing pillows and tables during the day, not to mention polishing his shoes and brushing his coat every morning, he is much more generous than if he had been on the car only a few hours and had not asked for any special service. Unless the trip is long he never gives more than a dollar. Twenty-five cents is the minimum.

By Automobile. From an economic point of view this problem has come to be almost as large as the railroad problem, and the part the automobile, including trucks and taxis, plays in business is growing larger and larger every year.

Motorists have a code of their own. They—when they do as they should—drive to the right in the United States, to the left in certain other countries. They take up no more of the road than is necessary, and they observe local traffic regulations scrupulously, not only because they will be fined if they do not but because it is impolite in Rome to do other than the Romans do. They hold out their hands to indicate that they are about to turn, they slow down at crossings, and they sound their horns as a warning signal but never for any other reason.

It is often necessary for a man who is trying to sell a piece of property to take out to look at it the man who thinks he will buy it. Needless to say, it is the former who pays for the trip. Other business trips are arranged by groups, the benefit or pleasure which is to result to be shared among them. Under such conditions it is wise (and polite) for them to divide expenses. These matters should be arranged ahead of time. If one is to furnish the machine, and one the gasoline, and another is to pay for the lunch, it should be understood at the outset.

In a Small Town. The salesman is now completely out of the metropolitan district. He is in a small town like hundreds of others over the United States. The hotel is very good in itself, but compared with the one in the city, which he has just left, it is inconvenient. He has better judgment than to remind the people of this. Instead, when he is talking to them—and he likes to talk with the people in the towns he is serving—he talks about what they have rather than what they have not and about what they can do in the future rather than what they have failed to do in the past. It is in this way that he discovers how he can best be useful to them.

He likes to work at the quick pace set by the big cities but he knows it will not do here. He goes around to see Mr. Carter. Mr. Carter is glad to see him, but he has had a bad year. The crops have not been good, the banks have not been generous, his wife has been sick, and one of his children has broken a leg. The salesman listens sympathetically to this tale of woe, leads the conversation away from the bad year behind to the good year ahead, and in a little while they are eagerly discussing plans for business in the next month or so. The salesman shows how he can help, and convinces Mr. Carter that the best time to begin is right now and gets an order for supplies from him. It has taken the better part of the morning, and Mr. Carter asks him to go home with him to lunch. The salesman would prefer going back to the hotel, but he knows that it will give Mr. Carter great pleasure to have him—his invitation is unmistakably hearty—so he accepts.

Before he came the salesman had discovered, through consulting the directories and by talking with friends of his who knew the town, who were worth going to see and who were not. Mr. Carter he had learned was immensely worth while and that is why he was willing to spend so much time with him. No salesman can afford to stop and talk with everybody who can give him the inside story of why business is no good. This salesman always finds out as much as possible about a man before he goes to see him. He never leaps blindly ahead when there is any way to get a gleam of light first.

Once in South Carolina he was anxious to get a large order from a wealthy old man who, he felt sure, would be a regular customer if he could once be persuaded to buy. The old man paid no attention to what he was saying until he mentioned the picture of a hunting dog that hung above the desk. The old man's eyes kindled. This was his hobby and he forgot all about business while he talked about hunting, and ended by asking the salesman to go home with him and spend the night. The salesman accepted gladly, and the next morning they went rabbit hunting instead of going back to the office. The salesman was out of practice in handling a gun but it was great fun, and the upshot of it all was that he "landed" the order he wanted.

This method is pleasant but wasteful. The salesman never uses it except as a last resource.

Much of the success of this salesman (and of the others who are successful) lies in the fact that he can put himself so completely into the place of the man he is trying to sell. He talks in terms of that man's work, and he tries to sell only where he believes the sale will result in mutual satisfaction. He never says anything about serving humanity, but his life is shaped around this idea, which is, when all is said and done, the biggest idea that any of us can lay ourselves out to follow.

He is working for a firm that he knows is honest—no self-respecting man will work for any other kind—and he wants its financial rating to stand solid. He does not sell to every man who wants to buy. He investigates his credit first, and if there is to be a delay while the investigation is under way he frankly tells the man so, and assures him that it is for his protection as well as for that of the house that is selling the goods. "It is a form we go through with every new customer," he says. "If we did not we'd find ourselves swamped with men who would not pay. And that would work hardship on those who do." Every business man knows that this is the only way in which reliable business can be carried on. And it is reliable business that we are interested in.

XIII

TABLES FOR TWO OR MORE

A YOUNG banker from Smithville is in New York. It is his first trip.

You would like him if you could see him. Tall, sun-burned, clean-cut, well-dressed, thoroughly alive and interested in everything. He is a bit confused by the city but he is determined to learn everything that it has to teach him. He does not hesitate to ask questions but he likes to find out without, whenever possible.

He goes into the dining room of the great hotel where he is staying, and for the first time in his life is confronted with an array of silver on both sides of his plate. At home he always has a knife, fork, and spoon laid together at the right of his plate, by which you can see that he has not lived among people who place much emphasis on having food daintily or correctly served. He is not exactly prepared for this. When he left Smithville he was thinking more of his business connections than of what he was going to eat, and how. He is embarrassed because, like every sanely balanced person, he likes to do things as they should be done, and not just blunder through them.   There is no one he can ask except the waiter, and the waiter seems such a superior person that he is afraid to ask him (though it would have been perfectly correct for him to do so).   He gets through the meal the best way he can and finds that when the ice cream is brought the only thing he has left to eat it with is a slender fork with a long handle and three very tiny prongs.   He knows that he has tripped up somewhere along the line, but he asks the waiter to bring him a spoon (he should have asked for a fork) and goes ahead.

The next day he is invited out to dinner with a man who has all of his life been accustomed to first-class hotels and restaurants and the dining tables of wealthy and cultured people.   He is somewhat older than our young banker and he has had a great deal of experience in entertaining men who have come into the city from small towns.   He is thoughtful, sympathetic, an excellent host.   He leads the way into the dining room (though they stand together in such a way that it seems that neither is leading) and chooses a table.   This nearly always means accepting the one the head waiter indicates, though it is quite correct for the host to suggest the table he would like to have.

"Does this suit you?" he asks the young banker before they sit down.

It suits him exactly. He says as much.

"Now, what will you have to eat?"

The waiter has given him a menu card, containing, so it seems to the young man, a million things that he might have. A dinner served in courses was something beyond his knowledge until the night before, and the dinner then was *table d'hôte* instead of *à la carte.* He flounders through the card and is about ready to thrust it aside and say, "Just bring me some ham and eggs" when his host sees his predicament.

"Blue Points are usually good at this time of the year," he says. "Shall we try them?"

The young man has not the remotest idea what Blue Points are but he thinks it will be very delightful to try them.

"What kind of soup do you like?" the host continues when the waiter has departed. "I see they have vegetable soup and consommé."

The young man clutches at the familiar straw. He will have vegetable soup.

Throughout the meal the host makes comments and suggestions and guides his guest through to the end, and does it so graciously that the young man from Smithville is not aware that he is doing it, and feels that it is all due to his own quick observation that he is getting along so well.   No business man is a perfect host until he can accomplish this.

Our young man knows already that one should sit up at a table and not lean forward or lounge back, that he should not take large mouthfuls and that he should not snap at his food, that he should eat without noise and with great cleanliness.   He knows that his napkin should be unfolded (it should be unfolded once and not spread out) and laid across his lap, not tucked into his collar or the top of his vest.   He knows that he should not eat with his knife.

He has never seen a finger bowl before but he has heard of them, so that when one is placed before him he knows that he should dip the ends of his fingers into it and dry them on his napkin. He has also heard that toothpicks are never used by gentlemen, at least in public, and he is not surprised when he does not see them.

He has read somewhere that when a knife or a fork is dropped to the floor he should not pick it up himself but should allow the waiter to do so, and that the waiter should be allowed to clear away the damage when something is upset on the table.   He knows that long apologies are out of order anywhere, and he is not likely to say anything more than "Excuse me" or "I beg your pardon" if he should by a clumsy movement break a glass or overturn a plate of soup.

But he does not know about the various knives and forks or about how courses are arranged, and he does not know about tips.

It is correct for him to explain to his host, just as Pip did when he was dining for the first time with Herbert Pocket, that he is unused to such things and beg him to give him a few hints as they go along. But it is less embarrassing to consult a book of etiquette about fundamentals and to pick up the other knowledge by close observation.

He discovers—our young friend uses both methods—that knives are laid at the right of the plate in the order in which they are to be used, beginning at the outside, and that the spoons are laid just beyond the knives in the same order. The butter knife (which rarely appears at dinner time) is usually laid across the little bread plate at the left of the dinner plate. Forks are placed at the left of the plate in the order in which they are to be used, except the oyster fork, which is laid across the knives or else is brought in with the oysters. The steel knife is for cutting meats. The flat fork with the short prongs is for salads.

Salads are always eaten with a fork. It is sometimes not very easy to do, but it is the only correct way.

This is the general standard, but there are deviations from it. Nothing but experience in dining—and a great deal of it—will teach one to know always what fork or what knife or what spoon to use when the table service is highly elaborate. The best policy for a stranger under such conditions is that of watchful and unobtrusive waiting.

The dinners that business men choose for themselves are rarely divided into numerous courses. Often they have only two: meat and vegetables, and desert. The regular order for a six-course dinner is: first, an appetizer such as oyster cocktail, grapefruit, strawberries, or something of the sort, followed by soup, fish, meat and vegetables, salad, dessert, cheese and crackers. One or more of the courses is often omitted.

The rule for tipping is universally the same: Ten per cent. of the bill.

Suppose the cases had been reversed and the man from the city had been in Smithville to take dinner with the young banker.

He is not accustomed to seeing all of the food put on the table at one time, nor to having to use the same fork throughout the meal. But he is a gentleman. He adapts himself to their standard so readily that not one of the people at the table could tell but that he had always lived that way.

The young banker is a gentleman, too. When his friends from the city come to visit him he gives them the best he has and does not apologize for it. He does not begin by saying, "I know you are used to having better things than this but I suppose you can stand it for one meal." He simply ushers his guest into the dining room as cordially and with as little affectation as if he were the paying teller of the Smithville bank. No one need ever apologize when he has done or given his best.

It is interesting to know that the standard of our young banker is growing higher and higher all the time. He likes to know how the people who have had time to make an art of dining do it and to adapt his ways to theirs whenever he can.

It is a grave mistake for a business man to feel that he must entertain another to the standard to which the second is accustomed. A poor man who finds himself under the necessity of entertaining a rich one should not feel that he must do it on a grand scale if he has been so entertained by a rich one. Aside from the moral question involved the great game of bluff is too silly and vulgar a one for grown men to play.

But business men play it and their wives join in. Suppose Mrs. Davis, whose husband is an assistant of Mr. Burke, wishes to invite Mrs. Burke to her home to dinner. She and Mr. Davis have been formally entertained in the other home, and the dinner they had there was superintended by a butler and carefully manipulated by two maids. Now Mrs. Davis has no maid, her china is very simple, and the food that she and her husband have, even when they entertain their friends, is plain and wholesome. Should she, for the great occasion, hire more beautiful china and engage servants? Should she draw on the savings bank for more delicate viands?

To begin with, Mr. Burke knows exactly what salary Mr. Davis gets. He knows whether it will warrant such expenditure. Will it make him feel like placing more responsibility on his assistant's shoulders to see him living beyond his means? Is it not, after all, much better for people to meet face to face instead of hiding themselves behind masks? The masks are not pretty, and in most cases deceive only the persons who wear them.

Men who are friends in business often like their wives to be friends as well. It is many times possible to bring about a meeting at the home of a common friend, but when this is not convenient, one of the women may invite the other. If the invitation is to dinner, it is not correct for Mr. Gardner to invite Mrs. Shandon even if he knows her and his wife does not. The invitation should go from Mrs. Gardner and should be addressed to Mr. and Mrs. Shandon. If the invitation is for tea, Mrs. Gardner simply invites Mrs. Shandon, and the nature of the invitation depends upon whether the affair is formal or informal.

As to which of two women should proffer the first invitation there might be some discussion. Usually it is the wife of the man whose position is superior, if they both work for the same concern. It frequently happens that a man whose position in business is high is married to a woman whose social standing is not of corresponding importance. Perhaps such a man has a subordinate whose wife is a social leader. In this case which of the women should extend the first invitation?

Most women of eminent social rank realize and appreciate the fact thoroughly. The social leader knows that the other woman might be embarrassed and hesitant about inviting her to her home. If she does apprehend this it is only gracious for her to extend the first invitation herself.

In small towns the rule is for the old residents to call upon the new, and the wife of a business man who has recently established himself in a community must wait until the women who live there have called upon her before she begins to entertain them.

In large cities where it is impossible to know everyone this rule is practically disregarded, and business men invite one another and ask their wives to do the same according to the way convenience and chance make most natural. Women whose husbands are longest in the employ of a firm, or whose husbands hold high positions, as a rule call first on the wives of newcomers or subordinates.

It all comes to the same thing whether it is in a city or a small town or the country. Those who are already established in the neighborhood or the business extend the right hand of welcome and good fellowship to those who are not.

In order to bring their employees together socially most big houses now give various entertainments such as picnics, parties, dances, and banquets. They are in no way different from other entertainments of the same kind so far as the etiquette of behavior is concerned. Formal dances and banquets in the evening require evening dress just the same, except with that very enormous group (to which most of us belong) who do not own evening dress. This does not mean that evening parties must be foregone by this group or that they should hire gala attire for the occasion, but simply that the men wear their business suits and the girls their "Sunday" dresses. It is just as correct, it is just as much fun, and it is infinitely wiser than giving a dollar down and a dollar a week for a *décolleté* gown or a swallow-tail outfit.

XIV

LADIES FIRST?

MOST girls who are in business are there to earn a living.

It is true that an increasing number of wealthy girls who are under no necessity to work but who want a definite place in the economic life of the world are entering business every year, but the great army of workers is made up of those who enter business because they are driven into it (driven, many of them, while they are yet very young), because it is the only way in which they can have their own money, or because it is the only way in which they can raise their standard of living.

The majority of business girls come from the homes of parents in moderate circumstances. They have had advantages—a high-school or a college diploma, a certificate from a business school, travel, specialized training—and all these they have added to their business capital. In many instances the opportunities they have had have not been brilliant, but every opportunity,

however small, carries with it the responsibility
to make the best of it.   Upon these girls, since
they outnumber the others and because they have
had advantages (a high-school education is an
enormous advantage if you are looking at it from
the point of view of a person who wanted one but
was not able to get it), rests the responsibility of
setting the pace for others.   And the standard
of behavior for the business girl, whether she be
rich or poor or in between, is the same.

The wealthy girls who enter business deliberately are usually followed by the same sensible
impulse that started them on their careers, and,
as a rule, they conduct themselves with dignity
and modesty.   The wealthy girls who, through a
turn of fortune have been forced into work and
have gone unwillingly, are another matter. "The
rudest girls we have," is the testimony of most
people who have to deal with them.   Conventional social charm and poise they may have but
they are without that finer sense of courtesy
which makes them accept whatever fate gives
them and make the best of it.   The fading
splendor of the days of plenty envelops them
like a cloud—remember that we are speaking of
the unwilling ones—they lose themselves in self-
pity, and the great fun that comes from good
work they miss entirely.

Many of the poor girls in business have never known anything but poverty, and their lives have been cast among people who have never known anything else. They have had no home training in the art of behavior (for the people at home did not know how to give it to them). No one has ever told them how to dress or act but there have never been lacking those to condemn them when they dressed foolishly or acted indiscreetly. "The silly little things," they say (and oh, how superior they are when they say it). Employers agree, for, after all, it is true, and the silly little things hold their jobs until they are married, until they are fired, or (and this happens frequently) until they wake up, and then they are promoted to something better. We cannot expect girls like these, who have grown up without contact with the gentler side of life, to begin with a high standard of behavior, but we can (and do) expect them, once they have been brought into touch with better things, to raise their standard. It is no disgrace for a girl to begin in ignorance and squalor; the disgrace lies in staying there.

First of all, the dress of the business girl. Most of the ill-breeding in the world is due to ignorance. Ignorance of the laws of beauty and taste causes one to make a display of finery, and over-dressing is a mark of vulgarity whether one can afford it or not.

The girl does not live—we believe this is right —who does not love pretty clothes. But the average girl does not have money to spend lavishly for them. Her salary, as a rule, is not princely, and there are often financial as well as moral obligations to the people at home. She cannot have Sunday clothes and everyday clothes. She must combine the two with the emphasis on the latter.

A few years ago it was almost impossible to accomplish this, but manufacturers have recognized her needs and are now making clothes especially for her—plain dresses in bright colors and dark dresses with a happy bit of trimming here and there, neat enough to pass the censorship of the strictest employer, pretty enough to please the most exacting young girl.

A woman is no longer thought eccentric if she wears low heels. The modern flapper is too sensible for such nonsense as French heels for standing all day behind the counter. Manufacturers have discovered this also, and are making shoes with low heels and broad toes quite as pleasing as the French monstrosities and infinitely more comfortable.

A business girl—or any girl, for that matter—

should take pains with her hands and her hair. Coiffures that might be appropriate in a ball room are out of place in an office, and heavily jeweled hands, whether the jewels are real or imitation, are grotesquely unsuited to office work. (So are dirty ones.)

Hair that is glossy and tidy, hands that are clean and capable, dress that is trim and inconspicuous—add to these intelligence, willingness, good health, and good manners and there is not much left to be desired.

Certain positions expose girls to the temptation of dress more than others. She, for instance, who all day handles lovely garments or she who all day poses before long mirrors in exquisite gowns that other women are to wear—can one expect these girls to go merrily home at night to a hall bedroom with a one-burner gas jet and a mournful array of old furniture? They have a problem that the girl in a glue factory or a fish cannery does not have to meet—at least not in so concrete a form. At the same time they have an opportunity that these other girls do not have, and it rests with them whether the opportunity or the temptation gets the upper hand.

Positions in which girls are thrown into close contact with men expose them to temptation of another sort. It is in its most acute form when it brings a poor girl into more or less intimate association with a rich man. Once, a very long time ago, a king married a beggar maid and they lived happily ever after. People have not stopped writing and talking about it yet, although it is many centuries since it happened. It is true that once in a very great while a girl marries her father's chauffeur or her brother's valet and finds later that she has acted wisely; but these are rare exceptions to the general rule, for the result usually is unhappiness. Such marriages are always the occasion for big headlines in the paper, usually a double set of them, for, in most instances, the divorce follows within a year or so.

It is a dangerous thing for a girl to receive attentions indiscriminately from men, especially those who drift across her horizon from the great world outside. It is dangerous (is it necessary to add that it is incorrect?) for a manicurist to accept presents from the millionaire whose hands she looks after. It is unwise for any girl to accept expensive gifts from a man who is not her fiancé.

There are exceptions to this rule, as indeed to every other. At Christmas or at the time a ceremony or an anniversary employers sometimes give their secretaries or another trusted employee a beautiful gift, and it is within the bounds of propriety for the employee to accept it. Often when he has been away from the office for several weeks a man presents his secretary a gift to express his gratitude for the capable way in which she has managed affairs in his absence, and this gift the secretary is privileged to accept. Gifts are seldom presented except where the association has been a long and highly satisfactory one.

But the girl who goes to the theatre with a man about whom she knows nothing except that he has the price of the tickets is running a serious risk. She is violating one of the most rigid principles of etiquette and she is skating perilously out beyond the line marked off by common sense. Nearly every man can, and does, if he is the right sort, present credentials before asking a girl if he may call or if he may escort her to a place of amusement. There are instances in romantic stories and in real life where a man and a maid have met without the help of a third party and have entered upon a charming friendship. They are rare, rarer in fact than in fiction. It is banal to say that a girl can usually tell. But she can, and if she has any doubt (and this is true of all her relations with men) she should have no doubt. She should stop where she is.

Where men and girls work together in the same building or in buildings near one another they often go to the same restaurant for lunch. It is natural that they should sometimes sit together at the same tables. It is correct for a man to sit at a table where there are already only girls (if the girls are willing), but it is not correct for a girl to sit at a table where there are already only men (however willing the men may be). In these mixed groups each person pays for his or her own lunch. It is not even necessary for the man, or the men, as the case may be, to offer to do so, and it is a distinct breach of the rules of etiquette for a girl to allow a man to pay for her lunch under such circumstances.

The only time when it is correct for a man and a girl who are associated together in business to have lunch, with him the host and her the guest, is when the engagement is made ahead of time as for any other social affair. On such an occasion he should be as attentive as he would in any other circumstances, taking care of her wraps and placing her chair if the waiter is not at hand to do it, suggesting dishes he thinks perhaps she will like, and making himself as

generally useful and agreeable as it is possible
for him to be.   A point about which considerable
breath is wasted is whether a man should enter a
restaurant with the girl following or whether
he should allow her to lead the way.   It makes
no material difference one way or the other, but
usually he permits her to go ahead and follows
closely enough behind to open the doors for her
and to receive whatever instructions the head
waiter has to offer.

If a man should enter a restaurant and find a
girl whom he knows already seated he may join
her if he thinks he will be not unwelcome, but
this does not make it incumbent upon him to pay
for her lunch.   He may offer to do it, but it is
a matter that rests with the girl.   If she does
not care to develop his acquaintance she should
not permit it, but if the two are good friends or
if she feels that he is a man she would like to
know,   she may give him her check to settle along
with his own.   A girl is herself the best judge
of what to do under such conditions, and if common sense does not show her the way out etiquette will not help.

Women in business sometimes bring up perplexing questions and create awkward situations.
Suppose a man has asked a girl several times to
a business-social lunch and she has accepted

every time.   It seems that she should, as a man would in the same position, make some return. If she works for a house where there is a dining room in which checks do not have to be settled at the end of every meal she may do so without the slightest difficulty, but if she is compelled to take him to a place where the check must be given to the waiter or paid at the desk before they leave, she must look out for a different way of managing things.   Business luncheons are usually paid for by the firm in whose interests they are brought about, and if the girl works for an organization where there are several men employed she may ask one of them to take her friend out to lunch.   Then, even if she is not present, her social duty is done.   The easiest way out of such a predicament, it is superfluous to say, is never to get into it.

A girl who enters business presumably accepts the same conditions that men have to meet.   She has no right to expect special favors because she is a woman.   She does get a certain amount of consideration, as indeed she should, but she is very foolish and childish if she feels resentful when a busy man fails to hold open a door for her to pass through, when he rushes into his office ahead of her, or when he cuts short an

interview when she has said only half of what she
had on her mind.

Much is said about the man who keeps his
seat on a train while a woman stands. His defense rests upon two arguments, first, that his
need is greater than hers (which is not true)
and, second, that she does not appreciate it even
when he does give it to her (which is not true
either). Unfortunately, there are as many rude
women in the world—and this statement is not
made carelessly—as there are rude men, and in
almost half the cases where a man rises to give
a woman his place the woman sits down without
even a glance toward her benefactor, as if the
act, which is no small sacrifice on the part of a
tired man, were not worth noticing. Every act
of civility or thoughtfulness should be rewarded
with at least a "Thank you" and a good hearty
one at that.

Old people, cripples, and invalids rarely fail
to secure seats, however crowded a car may be.
A man seldom offers his place to another man
unless it is evident that the other, because of age,
infirmity, or extreme fatigue is greatly in need
of it. Well-bred girls resign their seats to
old men, but if they refuse to accept, the
girls do not insist. At a reunion of Confed-
erate veterans several years ago a girl rose

from her place on a street car to allow a feeble old man to sit down. He gripped the strap fiercely.

"I ain't dead yet," he responded sturdily.

One of the chief petty complaints brought against women is that they do not keep their places in line. Some of them appear to have neither conscience nor compunction about dashing up to a ticket window ahead of twenty or thirty people who are waiting for their turn. Men would do the same thing (so men themselves say) but they know very well that the other men in the line would make them regret it in short order. Two or three minutes is all one can save by such methods and it is not worth it. Even if it were more it would still not be worth it.

When a woman breaks into a line it is quite permissible for the person behind her (whoever he or she may be) to say, "I beg your pardon, I was here first." This should be enough. Sometimes there is an almost desperate reason why one should get to a window. Many times everybody in the line has the same desperate reason for being in a hurry, but now and then in individual cases it is allowable for a woman (or a man) to ask for another person's place. *But only if there is a most urgent reason for it.* Much of courtesy is made up of petty sacrifices, and most of the great sacrifices are only a larger form of courtesy. It all comes back to Sir Philip Sidney's principle of "Thy need is greater than mine," but it is only extraordinary circumstances which warrant one's saying, "My need is greater than thine."

Since the beginning of time, and before (if there was any before) women have done their share of the work of the world. Formerly their part of it centered in the home but now that machinery has taken it out of the home they have come out of the home too, to stand in the fields and factories of industry by the side of their fathers and husbands and brothers. Because they have recently been thrown into closer association in their hours of work than ever before there has sprung up a certain amount of strife between men and women, and a great deal is said about how superior men are to women and how superior women are to men. It is pure nonsense. If all the men in the world were put on one side of a scale and all the women on the other, the scale would probably stand perfectly still.

The woman in business should never forget that she is a woman but she must remember that above all things she is a citizen, and that she her-

self has value and her work has value only as
they contribute to her community and her community as it contributes to her country. Courtesy is one of her strongest allies, this quality
which, alone, can do nothing, but, united to the
solid virtues that make character, can move
mountains.

We have said a good deal as we came along
about courtesy toward oneself and other people,
but perhaps the most valuable of all courtesies
in business is politeness toward one's job. It
is desirable for every woman to be pretty, well-
dressed, and well-groomed, but it is much more
desirable for the woman in business to be able
to do capable and efficient work. She may be
ornamental but she must be useful, and while
she is at the office her chief concern should be
with her job and not with herself. The end of
business is accomplishment, and courtesy is valuable because it is a means of making accomplishment easy and pleasant. It is this that gives
us the grace to accept whatever comes, if not
gladly, at least bravely.

It is a poor workman who quarrels with his
tools (or with his job), so the proverb says, and
there are two lines of Mr. Kipling's that might
be added. He was speaking of a king, but in
a democracy we are all kings:

The wisest thing, we suppose, that a king can do for
his land
Is the work that lies under his nose, with the tools that
lie under his hand.

And the lines are just as true when "girl" is
substituted for "king" and the pronouns are
changed accordingly.

THE END

CPSIA information can be obtained
at www.ICGtesting.com
Printed in the USA
LVHW100801211218
601328LV00012B/241/P